The
EMBROIDERED
CLOSET

MODERN HAND-STITCHING
FOR UPGRADING AND UPCYCLING
YOUR WARDROBE

Alexandra Stratkotter

ABRAMS, NEW YORK

For Oswald and Violet,
my greatest creations

And for my Omi,
who inspired my love of nature

And my Opa,
who showed me the value of hard work

contents

introduction 8

how to use this book 13

tools and materials 14

shopping list 20

transferring your pattern 21

stabilizers and interfacing 24

choosing fabrics for clothing embroidery 29

getting started 40

washing hand-embroidered garments 44

troubleshooting 45

a sustainable approach to fashion 46

thrifting 48

stitch guide 50

notes on mending 58

the projects 61

patterns 136

acknowledgments 156

about the author 159

introduction

My embroidery story began six years ago, when my son entered the world. At that time my hobby, and side hustle, was painting oil portraits, an art that doesn't lend itself well to rearing young children who don't really sleep. Often, during naptimes, I would get my palette and workspace prepped, and just as I began getting into the flow of painting, I would hear a cry from the other room. Those few spare moments didn't give me much time to paint, but I was still creatively fulfilled, which made me a happier person and a more attentive mother.

Then, when my son wasn't even two years old, he decided that napping just wasn't for him. With nap time cancelled, I found myself inadvertently trading paintbrushes for Play-Doh and portraits for playdates. Life eventually fell into a monotonous routine of stroller walks, laundry, and endlessly sweeping Cheerios off the floor.

Without a creative outlet, I grew restless for something to keep my hands busy. As I began to consider new crafts, embroidery unexpectedly caught my eye. I quickly fell down an Instagram rabbit hole and soon my screen was constantly flooded with images of wooden hoops that framed threaded florals, houseplants, swear words, pets, family names, and feminist affirmations. Instead of the delicate floral stitchwork I was accustomed to seeing at my grandmother's house, social media boasted images of embroidery designs

for absolutely anyone's tastes. This was a familiar art, but it felt modern and exciting. I wanted in.

When it comes to new crafts or hobbies (actually, life in general), I'm known for my impulsiveness. Embroidery was no exception. I dropped everything, bought out the entire needlecraft aisle of my local Michaels, and started stitching. My first embroidery hoop was a hot mess, but it didn't matter. I fell in love with the slow, meditative process, the sheen of the embroidery floss against the cotton, and the beautiful textures and combinations I could create with only a few simple stiches. The best part? How easily embroidery could be picked up and put down.

When a close friend of mine welcomed her second baby into the world, I lovingly designed a hoop with the name of her babe surrounded by a wreath of florals. In preparation, I watched countless YouTube videos, yet none explained how to stitch letters or how to convert a drawing into stitches. I made so many mistakes with this hoop, but I learned so much. My friend cried when I gave her the finished product, and I felt like I had arrived *home*. After posting a photo of the embroidery on Instagram, a friend asked me to make them a hoop. Then another friend. Then another. Soon I was charging for floral hoops, and six months later I started my online embroidery shop, Florals and Floss. As Florals and Floss has blossomed into a full-time creative business, I no longer

sell custom-designed pieces. I now spend my time teaching embroidery workshops, creating instructional patterns and kits, and browsing thrift shops for clothing to stitch on.

Like the rest of my embroidery journey, stitching on clothing also started with my son. He can wear through an item of clothing faster than he can grow out of it! I started mending small holes in his clothes with embroidered mushrooms, leaves, and other little woodland motifs that he calls "nature treasures." I was so pleasantly surprised by the social media enthusiasm over his embroidered clothing that I began experimenting on thrifted adult-size garments. I played with tapestry wool, different fabrics, and spent a whole lot of money buying all the wrong types of stabilizers. Through my experimentation, I've learned a lot about what works for clothing, what doesn't, and what ultimately doesn't matter.

I'm thrilled to share my love of embroidery with you through this book. The instructions will give you the confidence and the resources needed to take your embroidery further than just stitching hoops to be hung on a wall. I hope you'll be inspired to snuggle up on the couch with an audiobook or a TV show and begin stitching on your favorite T-shirt. In a fast-paced world, embroidery offers the chance to slow down and take pleasure in the process. Embroidery is about the destination, but also the journey. Enjoy.

This collection of projects will guide you through the complete process of embroidery and the intricacies of stitching on clothing, and they will give you a look at my creative process.

how to use this book

You'll learn how to add a little personal flair to your favorite dress, stitch beautiful botanical motifs on thrifted clothing, and breathe new life into that unloved shirt at the back of your closet.

In the initial chapters, you'll find all the basics. Whether you're a seasoned stitcher in need of a refresher or you're brand new to embroidery, I'll take you through all the necessary tools and materials and will show you how to transfer patterns, use stabilizers and interfacing, and choose the best garments for embroidery. Next, we'll focus on the most exciting part:

how to actually stitch on clothing! I'll offer my advice on thrifting as a way of responsibly sourcing clothing, the art of mending garments, and how to clean and preserve your newly embroidered clothes.

Each design is presented with a supply list, a stitch guide, and a color guide, and you'll find the corresponding patterns at the back of the book. If you need help with any stitches, you can refer to the stitch guide for step-by-step instructions.

Be creative, have fun, and remember— if you mess up, there's nothing a good pair of scissors can't fix!

tools and materials

It's been my experience that once you start telling people you've taken up embroidery, everyone you've ever known will offer you a box of their grandma's old embroidery supplies! If this doesn't happen to you, or you simply don't want to use a gifted shoebox of tangled threads, I've got you covered. Embroidery supplies are inexpensive and easily purchased online or in the needlecraft aisle of your local craft store or specialty fiber shop. If you're thrifty, you can usually find embroidery materials hanging around secondhand stores. You might even uncover some gems—all my prettiest antique embroidery hoops have been thrifted.

THREAD
There are a dozen different types of thread you can use for embroidery, ranging from thin to thick, dull to sparkly. The projects in this book are stitched with DMC brand cotton floss and tapestry wool.

Cotton Floss
Embroidery floss is cotton thread, made up of six small strands. You can use the full six strands or separate them for more detailed work. Cotton embroidery floss comes in hundreds of colors and is the easiest type of embroidery thread to find at your local craft store. Embroidery floss is usually used with an embroidery needle.

Tapestry Wool
Tapestry wool is thick, soft, and non-divisible. Because of its thickness, you can quickly cover a large area with embroidery. As tapestry wool is chunky and fluffy, you'll need a needle with a large eye, like a chenille needle, and you will likely need a needle threader to help guide your wool through the eye. I prefer using tapestry wool when embellishing sweaters or any type of thicker knit.

HOOPS
An embroidery hoop holds your project taut while you're working. It's important to use one in order to prevent puckering and wrinkles from forming around your stitches. While hoops come in a variety of materials, wooden or plastic hoops are ideal for stitching on garments.

How to Use an Embroidery Hoop

Separate the hoops by loosening the screw. Place your fabric over the inner hoop, trying to center your pattern as best you can, then place the outer hoop back over the fabric and inner hoop. Tighten the screw as you pull on all sides of the fabric to tighten evenly.

SCISSORS

You can use any type of scissors for embroidery, but small, sharp embroidery scissors will be your best friend. You'll also need regular all-purpose/craft scissors for cutting stabilizer, and a sharp pair of fabric shears if you're going to do any mending.

NEEDLES

The thread you choose determines which type of needle you'll work with.

Embroidery Needles

Embroidery needles have a larger eye than your standard sewing needle and come in a variety of sizes. The lower the number, the larger the needle and eye. A size 5 needle is a good choice when using cotton embroidery floss. If you find size 5 needles are challenging to thread, you can use a size 1.

Chenille Needles

A chenille needle has a larger eye than an embroidery needle, which makes it the perfect choice for thick threads like tapestry wool. I prefer size 22.

Needle Threader

Needle threaders are handy little tools to help guide your thread through the eye of a needle. While optional for cotton floss, you'll need one when using tapestry wool.

PATTERN TRANSFER TOOLS

Before you can begin stitching, you'll need to transfer your pattern to your garment. You can do this a number of ways: Trace the pattern with a pen/pencil or heat erasable marker, or use transfer paper or a stabilizer. See pages 21–23 for details on transfer tools and instructions on how to use them.

Writing Utensils

Writing utensils are the simplest tool you can use to transfer a pattern. You can draw or trace directly onto fabric with a marker, pen, or pencil. FriXion markers or pens are my personal favorites. They come in a variety of colors and the markings erase easily with a blow dryer. You can sometimes trace on dark fabric, but it has to be lightweight enough that the pattern can show through. White graphite or charcoal pencils work well, as do white Gelly Roll gel pens. But be warned, the ink from gel pens does not wash out!

Stabilizers

Stabilizers are a type of removable paper that you can stick or iron onto your garments. Different stabilizers accomplish different tasks: One can transfer a pattern to a dark or chunky knit garment while another can replace an embroidery hoop and keep stretchy fabrics taut so your embroidery won't wrinkle while working.

Stabilizers will be your go-to when stitching on clothing. See pages 24–26 for details on different types of stabilizers and how to use them.

Carbon Paper/Graphite Paper

This is a great transfer method for dark fabrics, or fabrics that are too thick for tracing, like denim. There are many types of carbon paper available at fabric stores. Alternatively, you can purchase graphite paper from art stores, which comes in black and white. I personally prefer graphite paper, as it doesn't smudge off as easily as the waxy transfer paper you will find in fabric stores.

RULER OR SEWING TAPE MEASURE

Rulers and other tape measures are helpful tools to have on hand when planning out your embroidery. You can use them to measure stabilizers before cutting or to evenly space repeating patterns. You don't need anything fancy! Any type of ruler, measuring tape, or sewing tape measure you have lying around is perfect.

OPTIONAL

Interfacing

Interfacing is a type of mesh that is permanently applied to fabric to add weight/structure to the fabric, or to protect the back of embroidery so you can wear and wash for years to come.

Thimble

You can use a thimble to protect your fingers while stitching. They are especially useful when stitching on thicker fabrics or layers of stabilizer, as your thumb can get sore.

Needle-Minder

Have you ever lost a needle in the couch cushions? Needle-minders are handy little decorative magnets that keep your needle safe and secure between stitches.

Iron

An iron can be used to smooth out lines in your clothing before stitching and to apply any materials that use a heat-activated adhesive. I'm admittedly unbothered by lines and wrinkles in my clothing, so when it comes to irons I typically don't use them for their intended purpose of smoothing fabrics (before or after embroidery). I do, however, use an iron when applying permanent interfacing to the back of my embroidery. My advice is to not run out and buy one, unless you come to a point where you feel an iron could be of use to you.

Sewing Pins

Sewing pins aren't a necessity for the majority of the projects in this book, but they come in awfully handy if you're mending or patching clothing.

shopping list

- DMC cotton floss
- DMC tapestry wool
- Embroidery needles (sizes 1–5)
- Chenille needles (size 22)
- Embroidery hoops:
    - 5-inch (13 cm)
    - 6-inch (15 cm)
    - 7-inch (18 cm)
- Embroidery scissors
- All-purpose/craft scissors
- Ruler or sewing tape measure

- Needle threader
- Transfer paper/pen/pencil
    - Pilot FriXion marker
    - White charcoal pencil or white Sakura Gelly Roll pen
    - Black/white graphite paper
    - DMC transfer paper
- Stabilizers/Interfacing
    - Sulky Sticky + tear-away stabilizer
    - Sulky Sticky Fabri-Solvy stabilizer or DMC Magic Paper
    - Sulky Tender Touch iron-on, "cover-a-stitch" stabilizer
- Optional
    - Thimble
    - Needle-minder
    - Iron
    - Sewing pins

transfer-ring your pattern

t he patterns in this book will need to be transferred onto your garment so you can start working. If you've been stitching for a while, you probably already have a favorite transfer method that works well for you. If you're just starting on your embroidery journey, here are some methods you can try.

In this book, I used a dissolvable stabilizer for every project. If you're new to embroidery and feel overwhelmed by the options, a dissolvable stabilizer would be my recommendation. While I'm a fan of using what you have (for example, pens and a window), a dissolvable stabilizer is easy and can be used on nearly any garment, which makes it worth the purchase.

LIGHT BOX OR WINDOW

When using a thin or lighter-colored fabric, I prefer to use a light source to trace the pattern. Fabrics such as cotton and linen tend to work best here as they can be more translucent. You can trace with any writing utensil you have handy.

How to Trace a Pattern Using a Light Box or a Window

Tracing an embroidery pattern is exactly how it sounds: Place the pattern inside the garment, hold it up to a window or light box (a bright computer screen or tablet works well), and trace the design.

If you have issues with your fabric moving around, you can hoop your fabric and use the inside of the hoop for tracing. Using the inside of a hoop allows the area you're drawing on to lie perfectly flat against the pattern. Start by turning your garment inside out and placing it onto your hoop. Pull the fabric taut from all ends. Center the hoop on top of your pattern (right side of fabric and inside of hoop facing you). Hold your hoop and pattern up to a light source and trace your pattern. Then remove the garment from the hoop and flip the garment so that the traced pattern is facing out. When you embroider the traced pattern, make sure to center it in the hoop as best you can by pulling the fabric in all directions.

How to Trace a Pattern Using Carbon/Graphite Paper

Transferring your pattern with carbon/graphite paper is pretty straightforward. Place your garment on a hard surface and then lay your carbon paper on top (graphite side touching the fabric). Lay your pattern over the carbon paper and, pressing firmly, trace with a pencil or pen. The color should transfer exactly where you pressed with the pen. If the white carbon paper doesn't show up as boldly as you would like, you can draw over your tracing with a white charcoal pencil or gel pen.

DISSOLVABLE STABILIZER

Dissolvable stabilizers make for an easy pattern transfer method when stitching on a dark fabric, or when a garment is too thick or loosely woven for other transfer methods. (A loosely knitted chunky sweater, for example, typically can't be traced onto.)

These stabilizers are easily applied to clothing using their sticky backing, and they dissolve with warm water when you're finished working. See pages 25–26 for detailed instructions on using a dissolvable stabilizer.

A NOTE ON LEFTOVER PATTERN-TRANSFER MARKS

When you finish stitching, sometimes you can still see markings on the fabric from your pattern transfer materials. (Black graphite is especially guilty of this.) To remove any leftover markings, you can gently wash your fabric, or you can spot clean using a damp cloth mixed with colorless laundry soap. I personally don't bother—marks and imperfections set your stitching apart from embroidery that's been mass-produced by machines and computers!

For example, a few years ago, my grandma passed down some linens she'd hand-embroidered when her kids were young. My favorite is a wheat-colored decorative tablecloth, adorned in florals. I bring it to all my markets as a table cover and it gets loads of compliments! If you take a close look at the embroidered florals, you'll see spots where a blue water-soluble marker still faintly remains around her stitches. I look at it as a little reminder of the love and care that went into her art.

stabilizers and interfacing

WHAT IS A STABILIZER?

Simply put, a stabilizer is a removable paper that keeps your garment stable while stitching. If you're stitching on a particularly stretchy item of clothing without some way of keeping it taut, you'll end up with puckered and wrinkled fabric around the embroidery. Stabilizers are also particularly useful when stitching on non-stretchy garments that are too thick to be put into an embroidery hoop (e.g., knitwear or thick jeans). Another great reason to use a stabilizer is to transfer a pattern to a dark or thick garment.

Note: There are many different stabilizers on the market. Some have a sticky backing, some need to be sewn onto fabric, and others require a temporary glue to stick. I say, opt for the sticky backing!

WHAT IS INTERFACING?

Interfacing is a permanent mesh that is ironed on to the wrong side of fabric to add weight or structure. Another popular way to use interfacing is to iron it onto the back of embroidery, as a soft layer against the skin (you see this used a lot with machine-embroidered children's garments), or to protect the embroidery through years of washing and wearing.

DO I REALLY NEED A STABILIZER?

You don't always need a stabilizer when stitching on clothing. You can easily transfer a pattern onto many types of garments by tracing or using transfer paper, and many types of fabrics can be stitched in a hoop without the need for reinforcement. But certain types of fabrics will require a little extra help. If you're brand new to embroidery and stabilizers feel overwhelming to you, or you're still building your supply collection, that's okay! You can always start a project using a light-colored garment for easy pattern tracing, and choose a fabric that won't need reinforcement, like cotton or linen. (For fabric-specific tips, see pages 29–38.)

WHICH STABILIZERS DO I ACTUALLY NEED AND HOW DO I USE THEM?

There are many types of stabilizers and interfacing available these days. All perform different tasks and can be applied in different ways. Through trial and error, I've settled on three products as my personal favorites. Two are stabilizers that can be used together—one is placed on the outside of your garment for pattern transfer, the other is used inside to add stability. Finally, there's the option of permanent interfacing, which adds durability and comfort when applied to the back of your finished embroidery.

If you aren't new to sewing or needlecraft, you may already have some favorite stabilizers, and that's great! My number-one advice with embroidery is do what you like and use what you have.

Sticky, Dissolvable Stabilizers

Use a dissolvable stabilizer as a pattern transfer method when stitching on a dark fabric, or when a garment is too thick or loosely woven for other transfer methods. These stabilizers are easily applied to clothing using their sticky backing, and they dissolve with warm water when you're finished working.

• Product Recommendation: **Sulky Sticky Fabri-Solvy Water-Soluble Stabilizer or DMC Magic Paper**

How it works:

1. Trace your design from the book onto the stabilizer.
2. Cut around the design. Leave an inch (a few centimeters) of space

around the outline as this will help anchor the stabilizer in place when you're stitching.

3. Peel off backing and stick onto fabric.
4. When finished stitching, rinse away the stabilizer by holding the embroidery under a running tap with warm water. Sometimes the sticky stabilizer doesn't completely wash away. If this is the case, simply agitate the stabilizer with your fingers or let it soak in your sink for a few minutes.

Sticky, Tear-Away Backing Stabilizers
A tear-away stabilizer is used on the inside of a garment that has a lot of stretch or is too thick to be placed in an embroidery hoop. The stabilizer acts as a hoop replacement and reinforces the fabric. This prevents stretch while working, so your finished product doesn't feature fabric that's wrinkled and puckered around the edges of your embroidery.

When you're finished embroidering, simply wet the stabilizer and tear it off your garment. You can try to remove any remaining stabilizer under the embroidered areas, but I personally don't bother, since backing stabilizer tears away best when wet and will eventually dissolve/come off after multiple washings.

• Product Recommendation: **Sulky Sticky + Tear-Away Stabilizer**

How it works:
1. Measure the design you're going to stitch and cut your stabilizer so it's a couple inches (5 cm) larger than the design. If using dissolvable stabilizer on the outside of your garment, cut the tear-away backing so it's the same size or even larger. This will ensure proper tension for your fabric.
2. Turn your garment inside out. Peel off backing and stick the stabilizer on the inside of your garment, centered behind your pattern.
3. When finished embroidering, wet stabilizer and tear away excess.

SOFT-TOUCH INTERFACING

Soft-touch interfacing is a soft, mesh-like material that is permanently ironed onto the back of a finished embroidered garment. It fuses with the embroidery to keep stitches and knots in place, and it protects against general wear and tear. When ironed directly over the wrong side of the embroidery, it acts as a barrier between the embroidery and the skin, which is especially useful for kid's clothing or for people with wool sensitivities (when you use tapestry wool).

• Product Recommendation: **Sulky Tender Touch Iron-On Backing**

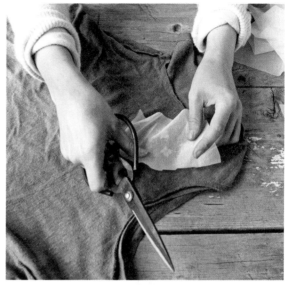

How it works:

1. Turn garment inside out and place interfacing over the back of the finished embroidery. Trace around the edges of the embroidery.
2. Cut the interfacing, leaving ½ inch (1.3 cm) of space around the area you just traced.
3. Place interfacing over the back of the embroidery and iron to adhere.

choosing fabrics for clothing embroidery

You can embellish any type of clothing with embroidery, but you'll have the most success with fabrics like cotton, linen, denim, and certain types of knitwear. However, not all fabrics are created equal, and even the quality among one type of fabric will vary greatly from garment to garment. To keep things simple, I have three fairly basic rules for choosing a garment to stitch on. First, choose a quality garment. "Quality" is highly subjective when it comes to clothing, but certain traits will help you assess which garments and fabrics are ideal for embroidery. Holes and tears can be mended, but a quality garment should have a well-constructed infrastructure, be made of durable fabrics, and utilize fabrics that are situationally appropriate. (A summer outfit with a breathable fabric, like linen, will be far more comfortable in hot weather than stuffy polyester.) Note that quality doesn't mean expensive. I have ten-dollar T-shirts that have lasted years longer than others that were five times the price. Quality boils down to how long a garment will last, how it feels against your skin, and how you feel when wearing it.

My second, and most important, rule for choosing a fabric is to avoid stretch. Having some elasticity to your clothing is absolutely no problem—a little bit of stretch can easily be remedied by the use of a stabilizer on the back of the fabric. But very stretchy fabrics are not ideal. Too much stretch will pull on your embroidery to create puckering and wrinkles along the outer edges. What's worse, if your fabric is too stretched while working, it will relax when finished and your embroidery will come loose and undone. Test your garment simply by pulling on it. If it stretches quite far, you may want to choose a different garment for embroidery.

Finally, think about the clothing you already own and consider upgrading and mending with embroidery before purchasing new garments. Let the fabrics and fibers of your own wardrobe guide your creativity. If you're feeling unsure about what garment to stitch on, run your hands along the clothing hanging in your closet and choose an item that *feels* good to you. If you need some technical advice, you can always check the tags on your garment and reference this handy guide to working with my favorite fabrics for embroidery.

NATURAL FABRICS

Cotton

Cotton fabric is a favorite among embroiderers and for good reason. It's a natural, woven fiber that is soft, breathable, affordable, easy to wash, strong (when high quality), and almost effortless to stitch on. Cotton is an extremely popular fiber choice for apparel and is found in a wide variety of clothing, especially "basics" like denim, tees, jackets, undergarments, socks, and even shoes and bags. Of course, no fabric is perfect. One hundred percent cotton is prone to shrinkage, which is why you should always wash and preshrink any cotton garments before doing any stitch work.

While 100 percent cotton comes in varying thicknesses, thicker cotton garments are best. This is not only for embroidery, but for the longeviy of the garment. As you move up the price chain of cotton clothing (e.g., ten dollars vs. thirty dollars) you'll find different weights and added

benefits. Cheap cotton apparel isn't the best choice for embroidery, as it's loosely woven, which makes it see-through and prone to holes and creases. You can buff it up with permanent interfacing but it likely won't be worth your time to stitch on it. The last thing you want is to be poking holes into fabric that's already susceptible to them! Pricier cottons are tightly woven, which makes them softer, heavier, and thicker. Additionally, a thicker cotton will hold its shape and will last longer.

Cotton blends can also be really lovely to stitch on and can giv additional structure to the weave. (Cotton-linen and cotton-polyester are common blends.) Certain blends will add significant elasticity to your garment (e.g., cotton-rayon), but you can counteract the added stretch with the use of stabilizers.

Linen

Linen is a natural fiber made from flax, which is extremely breathable, moisture-wicking, and quick drying (aka a great fiber for sweaty days). It's also antibacterial and, as a huge bonus, is environmentally friendly. Linen possesses a stunning texture that starts out feeling stiff, but gets softer with use. And since it's an exceptionally strong fabric, you'll find linen garments will outlast others in your collection.

While it relaxes (marginally) with wear, linen has no stretch, which makes it perfect for embroidery. The downside is you

have to ensure a good fit with a new-to-you garment, since there's no elasticity. It's also the wrinkliest fabric on the planet! I personally don't mind wrinkles in my clothing, but if you do, I would trade a few of the benefits of linen and opt for a linen-cotton blend, which will wrinkle far less.

If you're looking to purchase pure linen apparel, you're not likely to find much selection in your local department store. Luckily, the slow-fashion and artisan markets for linen clothing and homeware provide a multitude of options. If handmade linen clothing is out of your price range, you'll be happy to know it's a fabric found abundantly in thrift stores.

Denim

Used primarily to make jeans, denim is an easily embroidered textile made of cotton or cotton that's been blended with another fiber to add stretch. Durability and sturdiness will increase with the amount of cotton found in denim, but you will lose give to the fabric. The ideal fiber content of your denim really depends on the type of garment you choose. For example, a denim shirt doesn't require much stretch, so 100 percent cotton is great for fit and breathability, and it works beautifully for embroidery. (Just make sure to wash it first because o shrinkage.) Alternatively, a pair of skinny jeans needs elasticity for a good fit, so an addition of spandex adds necessary stretch to the jeans while allowing the knee and bum areas to "bounce back"

into place after movement—no one likes it when their jeans sag! Typically, raising the spandex ratio too much will result in more stretch, thinner material, and a shorter lifespan—all of which are bad for embroidery. For comfort and ease of stitching, I like a jean with a ratio of 2–5 percent spandex and the rest cotton. It's very much a personal preference. If you like a stiff denim garment, you'll have an easier time stitching on it. If you like a very stretchy denim, that's okay too. Just stabilize to offset the elasticity and treat the garment with care so it can last longer. *Note:* Denim that's been dyed with dark indigo can bleed. The last thing you want is your beautiful handiwork turning blue! If you're stitching on a new-to-you dark-colored denim, make sure to give it a good rub with your hands. If any blue transfers to your palms, wash the denim by itself, inside out, on a cold water setting in your washing machine. After washing, if the garment is still transferring color, you can try soaking the denim in a gallon (3.8 L) water with a mixture of ¼ cup (60 ml) vinegar plus two tablespoons salt to set the color, then give it another good wash.

Chambray

Chambray is a natural fabric that's similar to denim, in both look and construction. It's made of cotton, which makes it breathable and light, and it is typically found in button-down shirts or as a lightweight denim replacement in garments like jackets, pants, and shoes. Chambray, being made of cotton, is exceptionally easy to embroider on. Just make sure to remove any dark indigo dyes and to preshrink the cotton by giving it a wash before stitching.

Wool

Throughout history, wool has been an advantageous clothing choice for its warmth, breathability, durability, and self-cleaning properties. Wool is made from sheared animal fur, and prominent wool varieties are labeled by the animal they are sourced from, like merino from sheep, cashmere and mohair rom goats, and angora from rabbits.

Wool has many features that make for a great item of clothing. However, as with most garments, the benefits depend on the quality. Cheap wool apparel is likely to pill, stretch oddly, and wrinkle easily. Unless you need the insulation or moisture-wicking properties wool provides, it's advisable to consider other fibers or a wool blend instead of cheap wool.

Stretch, the ever-important embroidery qualifier, isn't common in woven wool apparel (e.g., pants and coats), but when you're stitching on a wool blend, or a wool knit, you may find some elasticity. Make sure to give your wool garment a little tug to check the stretch and stabilize if necessary.

Before you begin embroidering on a wool garment, one of the most important things to know is that wool clothing must be handwashed and cannot be machine dried, or you'll face significant shrinkage. This is evidenced by the drying devastation of 2015, when my husband accidentally turned my favorite wool sweater into a crop top. In retrospect, I think it may have been a small mercy. The itch I felt when wearing that sweater can only be compared to the feeling of sandpaper grinding into my skin.

Turns out, thick wool is a common irritant for many people, because the rough ridges and coarse fibers rub against the skin and make you feel itchy. The finer the fiber, the less you'll feel the edges rubbing against your skin.

Many people are allergic to wool itself and will have no reprieve regardless of fiber size. Wool allergies typically come from the lanolin in the wool (a naturally occurring wax found in the fur, which is also used in many face lotions and body creams). Lambswool and alpaca are both free of lanolin, but if you have issues with animal fur in general, it's advisable to stick to synthetics or other fibers.

Sheep fur is the most prevalent in wool varieties. If a garment is labeled only as "wool," it is likely sheep's wool and not very high quality. High-quality wools typically are labelled by the animal they come from, and the animals boast differences in fiber size: The finer the fibers, the softer the garment. While the thickness or softness can differ from fiber to fiber, the amazing benefits of wool stay the same across the variances.

- **Merino** wool comes from merino sheep and is known for its quality. Compared to basic sheep's wool, merino fibers are much finer, which in turn makes merino garments a softer choice with a bit less shrinkage.
- **Cashmere**, a luxury fiber, is produced by cashmere goats. Cashmere fibers are extremely fine, which makes these garments softer, lighter, and more breathable than sheep's wool clothing. Cashmere does come with a price tag, but its durability means a long lifespan for your garment if properly cared for.
- **Mohair** comes from angora goats. Mohair is warmer than cashmere and sheep's wool, drapes nicely, and isn't prone to wrinkles. Mohair garments can either be silky-soft or extremely scratchy, so it's advisable to try them on if you're buying them new-to-you.
- **Angora**, not to be confused with the wool of angora goats, comes from angora rabbits. Angora wool is easily recognizable by its fuzziness, which gives it an ethereal texture and makes it extremely soft to the touch. It's common to find angora even in the smallest of quantities in knitted

garments (especially sweaters and outerwear accessories like scarves and hats), which can be problematic as it's a common irritant/allergen for those who are sensitive to wool or animal hair. Of all the wool varieties, this is the one I would recommend the least for embroidery, as angora sheds a lot, felts quite badly, and isn't durable.

- **Alpaca** wool is similar to sheep's wool, but it's warmer and less scaly (itchy). You'll find alpaca wool in knitwear, outerwear, blankets, and woven garments like suits or dress pants.

Silk

Silk, in a class of its own due to its gorgeous luster and ability to drape beautifully across the skin, makes for striking items of clothing. Because of silk's sheen, you'll commonly find it in women's garments like blouses, dresses, and lingerie, whereas for men it's usually only found in accessories like ties, suit linings, and underwear. A few benefits of this natural fiber are its strength and durability, wrinkle-resistance, and unbelievable softness. The downside to silk is that it's the highest maintenance fabric of all. It must be dry cleaned and it may need to be dry cleaned often because silk holds smells and doesn't breathe well in the heat. (It does make a good insulator in cooler weather.)

Silk garments work very well for embroidery as they are strong, don't stretch much, and will "bounce back" when

you're working. Because silk reflects light differently than most fabrics, depending on the garment you choose, you may want to consider silk embroidery floss instead of cotton floss.

SYNTHETIC FABRICS

Polyester

Polyester is a synthetic fabric made from petroleum, which can be challenging to stitch on due to its slippery texture, tight weave, and inability to "bounce back" like other fabrics. As with any fabric, there are different qualities of polyester. On one hand, many fast-fashion retailers (trendy and cheap clothing stores with fast product turnover) favor this fiber in their clothes to replace natural fibers, as it's cheaper and quicker to produce. These brands will typically create poly-garments that are thin, flimsy, and not made to last. On the other hand, polyester can actually be used to increase durability and hold shape when blended with natural fibers like wool or cotton. (These blends are common in higher-end clothing.) Polyester also offers the unique ability to create effects not possible with natural fibers, like making garments sheer or pleated. Because of its popularity among clothing retailers, it's likely you already have a polyester shirt hanging in your closet just waiting to be embellished. I'm a huge proponent of using what you already own. Don't let the drawbacks of polyester deter you! With a bit of additional care, it can absolutely be embroidered on.

A polyester blend, ideally a cotton-polyester combo, is by far the best choice for embroidery (and breathability). The lower the polyester ratio, the fewer compromises and reinforcements required. (Common ratios are 65 percent cotton and 35 percent polyester, or 50:50.) If you choose a garment that's mostly polyester, don't forget to stabilize to avoid leaving visible holes around your stitches. Think carefully about where to place your stitches so you won't need to cut out mistakes, and choose the smallest needle size with the fewest floss strands you are comfortable using.

Acrylic

Acrylics are synthetic fibers (usually found in knitwear such as sweaters) which are not all created equal. Some will feel scratchy and fray easily; others will feel smooth but will probably pill quickly. Acrylic is common in fast-fashion knitwear because it's a material that's inexpensive and quick to produce. Since acrylic won't stand up to wear and tear as well as other fibers, it's best to avoid 100 percent acrylic garments. (In my experience, acrylic blends are fine.)

SEMI-SYNTHETIC FABRICS

Semi-synthetics are typically easy to stitch on, as they are woven to emulate the feel of natural fibers like linen, silk, or cotton. The only drawback is stretch, which fortunately can be suppressed by the use of stabilizers. If you want to reduce stretch at a fiber level while giving your wardrobe a little treat, look for rayon garments blended with cotton or linen.

Viscose/Rayon

Viscose and rayon are two names for the same thing: a semi-synthetic fiber made from processed wood pulp. Multiple chemical treatments are used to break down the pulp's cellulose and reconstitute it into fibers. Rayon is absorbent and drapes well, but it tends to shrink when exposed to heat—a bit problematic for garment embroidery, but you can work around this by dry cleaning your clothing, or handwashing garments and laying them flat to dry.

Modal/Lyocell (Tencel)

Modal and lyocell (Tencel is the popular brand name for lyocell) are subcategories of rayon that are manufactured in a similar way. Modal is spun to be stronger and more flexible than traditional rayon. (And it can go in the dryer without shrinking!) Lyocell uses a different chemical solvent to break down cellulose and reuses the solvent, which makes it the most environmentally friendly option. Lyocell is affordable, as breathable as cotton, feels like silk, and drapes beautifully, which makes it one of my favorite fibers to wear.

getting started

You have your supplies, a pattern, and your favorite denim jacket. Now what? It's time to stitch.

1. WASH ANY NEW GARMENTS
Prewash all new garments, especially materials that are prone to color bleed or shrinkage.

2. TRANSFER YOUR PATTERN
Begin by transferring your pattern. (See pages 21–23 for instructions.) Consider the placement of your design and where it will work best on the clothing you've chosen.

3. HOOP OR STABILIZE YOUR PATTERN
If using a hoop, place your garment in the hoop and pull on every section of fabric to tighten evenly. Tightening clothing in a hoop is a bit of a balancing act: You want the fabric to be taut, but not too tight. It's something you'll definitely get a feel for once you start working. If you're unsure about the proper tension for your fabric,

a good rule is to try to have the fabric just a smidge tighter than how it would rest naturally.

For thick garments, like certain types of jeans or chunky knit sweaters, you won't be able to fit a hoop over the fabric. It's a bit more challenging to stitch without a hoop, however a layer of tear-away stabilizer at the back of your garment works well to keep your fabric taut.

For stretchy garments, use a tear-away stabilizer on the back while stitching. Cut the stabilizer larger than your hoop size and stick it on the area you will be stitching, then place garment in the hoop. This will keep your fabric from moving too much and help prevent hoop burn (see page 45). *Note:* Using stabilizer can be hard on your fingers! Use a thimble and save your poor thumb.

4. CHOOSING YOUR THREAD TYPE
It's best to choose your thread based on the texture of the garment you're about to embroider. For instance, if I'm stitching on a thinner material, like a cotton T-shirt or

a thinner knit, I'll typically choose cotton embroidery floss, as it's also thinner. If I'm going to stitch on a thic knitted sweater or something really loosely woven, I reach for a skein of thick tapestry wool. Linen is a magical fabric that can be embellished with any type of embroidery thread.

If using cotton floss, choose how many strands you want to use. Splitting floss into four strands will take longer but will typically yield smoother results than using a full six strands. I usually stitch with a full six; the floss just doesn't stay as flat and neat looking after washing. That's the trade-off for a puffy texture.

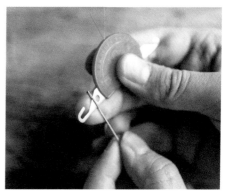

5. THREADING YOUR NEEDLE
The needle you choose depends on the type of thread you are working with. For some people, the hardest part of embroidery is threading their needle!

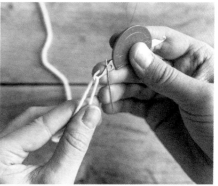

Threading a Needle with Tapestry Wool
When using tapestry wool, I recommend using a chenille needle, as it has a large eye. Tapestry wool can be challenging to thread because it's so fluffy, so I highly recommend using a needle threader.

To use a needle threader, put the large hook through the eye of your needle. Place the thread through the hook. Pull the hook back through the needle eye, which will pull your wool through too. Voilà!

Threading a Needle with Cotton Floss

When using cotton embroidery floss, I recommend using an embroidery needle. Trim the end of your floss so you're left with an edge that's clean and straight, then flatten the edge with your fingers. Pinching the cleanly trimmed tip of the floss between your thumb and index finger, guide the thread through the needle's eye.

If you're struggling to get all strands of floss through the eye, here's a little trick:

- Split your floss into half the number of strands you plan on using. For example, to use six strands split your floss into threes.

- Take the three strands and thread them through your needle. This is the hardest part. If you can't get the floss through the eye, you can use a needle threader for this.

- Bring your needle to the center of the floss.

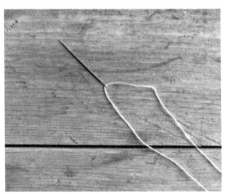

- Join both ends of the thread and knot them together, opposite the needle.

- By joining the split floss back together, you should now have the proper number of strands you want to work with.

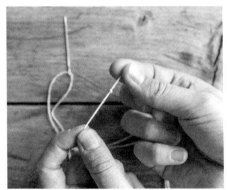

6. BEGIN STITCHING

Finally, the fun part: starting to stitch.

A few tips and tricks:

- You can begin anywhere on your pattern; there's no right or wrong way to stitch. I typically find it easiest to work from the biggest areas down to the smallest details.
- When doing embroidery as hoop art, it's common to knot the end of your working thread before starting your stitches. For garment embroidery, I prefer to knot the tail to my working thread *after* I start my first stitch. This keeps the knot from pulling through your clothing, especially when using tapestry wool on knitted garments.
- If using French knots, make sure to come up and go down through different spots on your fabric, so the knots don't pull through. This is especially important when stitching on loosely knitted fabrics.
- When you run out of floss or are ending a stitch, flip your garment to the back, split your floss in half, and make a couple knots. I like to make a knot, run my needle under a laid stitch, and then make one more knot. This ensures no knots will ever come undone in the wash.
- After you make the finishing knots at the back, snip off any excess thread. You don't want any extra threads to snag in the wash.
- If you're brand new to embroidery, watching YouTube tutorials and playing around is helpful.
- If you mess up at any point, there's almost nothing a good pair of embroidery scissors can't fix.

7. FINISHING YOUR GARMENT

When you are finished stitching, remove the hoop and any stabilizers. Double-check the back of your stitching to ensure there are no loose threads. If you want to keep your embroidery extra snug and secure, you can iron permanent interfacing onto the back of your stitching.

8. ENJOY WHAT YOU'VE CREATED!

Give yourself a high five! You've embroidered your first garment! Now, on to the next.

washing hand-embroidered garments

Once your garment is stitched, handwash (if possible) or use a gentle cycle on your machine. I prefer to wash my embroidery inside out as well, using cold water and unscented, uncolored laundry detergent. I always lay pieces flat to dry. Using permanent interfacing on the inside of your garment also helps keep your embroidery safe in the wash.

That being said, I'm exceptionally carefree when it comes to washing my son's embroidered clothing. I normally chuck his clothing in the wash multiple times a week, and I haven't had any issues with the look or integrity of the embroidery. Turns out embroidery can take a bit of abuse, so don't be too fearful of washing your work!

trouble-shooting

EMBROIDERY FLOSS IS FREQUENTLY KNOTTING

It's an unspoken embroidery rule that no matter what you do, your threads will knot or tangle every so often while stitching. I have very little patience for knots, which has resulted in a thirty-second rule: If I can't undo it in thirty seconds, I cut it off, re-thread my needle, and continue working.

If you find knots are becoming more frequent, use a shorter thread length. The longe thread you use, the more likely you are to have knots. If you're a beginner, two feet (61 cm) of floss is a good starting point. From there, you can increase or decrease the amount of thread until you find your preferred working length. Another way to prevent knots is to let your thread and needle occasionally unwind, either by hanging them upside down and letting gravity untwist the floss, or by simply pulling on the thread from the base to the tip so it straightens.

WRINKLES AND PUCKERING AROUND YOUR EMBROIDERY

Some puckering of the fabric around your stitching is absolutely normal. However, if wrinkles around your work become blatantly noticeable as you stitch, there are a few things you can check.

1. The fabric is either not tight enough in the hoop or it's pulled too tight (more likely the latter). Try to keep the fabric ying as naturally as it would if you were wearing it.
2. You're pulling too hard on your threads while stitching, which stretches the fabric and causes puckering.
3. Your garment is too stretchy and you may need to use stabilizer as reinforcement.

AVOIDING/FIXING HOOP BURN

Hoop burn is the term for a deep-set wrinkled ring that can be left on your fabric after you've removed an embroidery hoop. Farics that wrinkle easily tend to fall victim to hoop burn more frequently than other fabrics. The important thing to know is that hoop burn is typically not permanent and can easily be removed by ironing, steaming, or washing your garment. (I like to hang my garment in the bathroom while I shower to remove any hoop marks.)

To avoid hoop burn altogether, it's best to remove your embroidery hoop when taking a break from stitching. Another method that works exceptionally well is to use tear-away stabilizer on the back of your fabric. Make sure to cut the stabilizer larger than your hoop. This will keep the fabric from being "stressed" when you place the hoop over it.

IF YOUR THREAD BLEEDS COLOR WHEN RINSING AWAY DISSOLVABLE STABILIZER

If you are using quality embroidery threads and are rinsing your stabilizer in warm (not hot) water, you shouldn't experience any bleeding colors—most of the time! Even when you take all the precautions, threads will bleed on occasion. It actually happened to a sweater in this book! A white sweater, of course. When threads bleed color all you have to do is wash your garment with warm water and laundry detergent on a gentle cycle.

a sustainable approach to fashion

Since the mid-2000s the "fast fashion" industry has manufactured trendy clothing at warp speed. These clothes line the shelves of mass-market retailers, making these big companies millions of dollars in profits while the garment workers earn pennies. Fast fashion also comes at a huge cost to the environment. Most fast fashion garments are made of synthetic fibers, which won't break down in landfills. This is a problem because these garments are cheap in every sense of the word: Fast fashion is made to be discarded and to encourage repurchasing. This cycle of discarding and repurchasing clothing contributes to twelve million tons of textile waste dumped into North America's landfills each year.[*]

* "Clothes from Canada account for huge waste," *The National*, CBC, 2017, accessed December 16, 2021, www.cbc.ca/player/play/1140389443838; and Abigail Beall, "Why clothes are so hard to recycle," BBC, July 12, 2020, www.bbc.com/future/article/20200710 -why-clothes-are-so-hard-torecycle.

So, what's to be done?

Over the last few years, there has been a rapid trend toward ethical fashion and sustainability when it comes to shopping for clothing. But what does this mean exactly? To break it down simply: Ethical fashion focuses on reducing the industry's environmental impact, while creating and maintaining living wages and safe working conditions for the people who make our clothing. This, of course, is a very simple summary of an extremely complex issue.

It's becoming easier than ever to find ethical, slow fashion brands that create lasting garments using natural materials and fair labor practices. I have a few slow fashion pieces in my closet, all of which took me months to save up for. It's a privilege to be able to buy ethical clothing—a luxury that only a small percentage of the population can afford, which is why we should be focused on sustainability. Sustainability can mean simply taking care of the items you already own, buying less clothing overall (whether fast, slow, or secondhand fashion), buying fewer synthetic fabrics, and focusing more on purchasing items you don't have to frequently replace.

Of course, it's easy to say "take care of your clothes and stop shopping all the time!," when in reality we all get tired of our clothes, wear through them, or have gaps in our wardrobe for one reason or another. This is where embroidery comes in! Embroidery can update boring old shirts, stylishly mend ripped and damaged clothing, and breathe imagination into a trip to the thrift shop.

Most of the garments featured in this book have been purchased from slow fashion or secondhand retailers, borrowed, or taken from my own closet. Whatever you choose to stitch on, I hope this book can bring some sustainable inspiration to your own closet.

thrifting

thrifting is the most sustainable way to shop. Buying secondhand reduces the amount of clothing that ends up in landfills and saves water. (It takes around 1,800 gallons of water to grow enough cotton to produce one pair of jeans.) Thrifting also puts less money into the hands of companies that use child labor and sweatshops, or that don't pay living wages. Another bonus: It's inexpensive!

MY TIPS FOR SUCCESSFUL THRIFTING

- Thrifting takes time, and you'll need to be prepared to search. Make it a more relaxing experience by wearing comfortable clothing, and bring a water bottle and hand sanitizer.
- Go often! Some days you find some gems, some days you don't. It's okay to leave empty-handed.
- If you live in a city with multiple thrift shops, consider the neighborhoods they are located in when choosing where to shop. My favorite secondhand store is in a neighborhood surrounded by multiple trendy, up-and-coming neighborhoods.
- There is a difference between a big chain secondhand store and boutique thrift shops and consignment stores. The latter two will feature higher prices, but the clothes have been carefully vetted and curated for quality and aesthetics.
- For babies and very young children, I find it difficult to find clothing at bigger secondhand stores. Child-specific secondhand stores are your best bet.
- If you don't have brick and mortar thrift stores in your area, there are loads of online secondhand clothing shops and buy/sell websites.
- Big thrift shops release new clothing every day. Smaller shops may only put out new clothing once a week. It's completely fine to ask the staff what days they release new garments.
- If you are looking for a specific item, you are usually bound to be disappointed. Instead, shop with a general idea of what you're searching for, such as a new sweater or a pair of jeans. Or focus on colors or fabrics you'd like to add to your wardrobe. This will

help you fill gaps in your collection and keep you from buying items you won't wear.

- Search the racks outside of your size range. Items get misplaced and size varies drastically from brand to brand.

- It's been my experience that some of the best plain tees, sweaters, flannels, and cardigans are found in the men's section. This is because high-quality androgynous apparel (such as a large plain cotton tee) usually gets sorted into men's fashion.

- Focus on the quality of clothing and fabric instead of the brand.

- Buttons and zippers are a great way to measure quality. Metal zippers, and metal and wood buttons, almost always indicate better garment quality than clothing with plastic notions.

- Be sure to check that zippers work and that the buttons are all accounted for and firmly attached. Buttons can be reattached, but it won't do you any good if they fall off before you arrive home.

- I don't mind a bit of pilling on my sweaters, but a lot of pilling is a common annoyance to many people and can actually be a sign of a garment's short life expectancy. Look for pilling in armpits; on the shoulders of shirts, where people frequently touch hanging clothes; and in the thigh area of pants, where legs rub together. Some clothing, like a wool sweater, is going to have pilling no matter what, but a pair of jeans with substantial pilling in high-friction areas indicates they may not last long.

- Try things on. I have a rule for myself: If I don't absolutely love something in the dressing room, I likely won't wear it at home. Even if it's only five dollars. *Note:* Some smaller thrift shops don't have dressing rooms. In this case, shop in a tank, leggings, or shorts, so that you can try on clothes in public.

- It's inexpensive to have a tailor alter a quality garment so it perfectly fits your body, but only buy something to be altered if you'll actually have it done.

- Set a budget for tailoring. This will help you narrow down your options and cut down on purchases you don't need.

- If a piece of clothing is lovely but has an unsightly label, cover it with embroidery!

- Look for holes, stains, or other imperfections. Embroidery can turn an imperfection into a beautiful focal point, but you'll want to make sure the area is in a spot that makes sense to embroider. There's really no sense in putting hours of work into an armpit.

- Wash everything before wearing. You don't know where these items of clothing have been, or what they have been through. Wash. Everything.

stitch guide

Although there are hundreds of different embroidery stitches, over the years I've found myself gravitating toward a select few for my work. The stitches listed below, which are all popular in modern embroidery, are the stalwart stitches of my embroidery patterns. They are simple stitches, but when arranged in interesting combinations they create dynamic designs.

Every project in this book uses these stitches as a base. When you're working, come back to this chapter at any time for a stitching refresher.

STRAIGHT STITCH 50

BACKSTITCH 51

SPLIT STITCH 51

STEM STITCH 52

COUCHING 52

SATIN STITCH 53

LEAF SATIN STITCH 54

LONG AND SHORT STITCH 55

FRENCH KNOTS 56

DETACHED CHAIN STITCH 57

CHAIN STITCH 57

STRAIGHT STITCH

A straight stitch is the most basic and fundamental of all embroidery stitches. To place this stitch, simply bring the needle up from the back of the fabric where you want your stitch to start (A) and back down where you want your stitch to end (B). A straight stitch can be any length or direction.

A ———— B

BACKSTITCH

This is an invaluable stitch for linework on a project. In this book, you'll find it's used for stems, branches, and outlines.

Step 1. Decide where you would like to begin stitching your line. At your chosen starting point, bring your needle up through the fabric (A) and then bring it down through the fabric to make a straight stitch going forward (B). The length of your stitches doesn't matter, as long as you try to keep them spaced evenly.

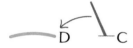

Step 2. Come up one stitch length ahead (C) and make a stitch backward, inserting needle where your previous stitch ended (D). The closer together you place your stitches, the cleaner your line will be. (You can even put your needle through the same exit hole from your last stitch.)

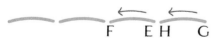

Step 3. Bring your needle up another stitch length ahead (E) and make a stitch backward, meeting where your last stitch ended (F). You can repeat the process, continuing to come up one stitch length ahead and placing a stitch backward, until your line is finished.

SPLIT STITCH

A split stitch is a simple stitch that can be used instead of a backstitch to embroider linework. By continuously "splitting" straight stitches in half, you'll create a thick and visually interesting line.

Step 1. At your chosen starting point, make a straight stitch going forward.

Step 2. Bring your needle up from the bottom of the fabric, in the middle of the stitch you previously placed. This splits the floss. Then bring your needle back down, one stitch length away.

Step 3. Continue to split each stitch from the bottom, moving along your pattern until your line is stitched.

STEM STITCH

If you need a whimsical alternative to a backstitch or split stitch, look no further than a stem stitch. The rope-like appearance makes it a great stitch for embroidering outlines, stems, and branches. Technique-wise it's similar to a split stitch, but you bring your needle from above the laid floss instead of through it.

Step 1. Place a single straight stitch. In the middle of the stitch, bring up your needle directly above the laid thread (A). Then bring your needle down through the fabric, one stitch length away (B).

Step 2. You should have two stitches overlapping. Just like you did before, bring your needle through the fabric directly above your previously laid thread, and then back down one stitch length away.

Step 3. Continue making stitches, bringing your needle up from the top of each previously placed stitch.

COUCHING

Couching is an embroidery method where you take a stitch and "pin" it in place using another stitch. It's very simple but extremely versatile. Couching can be used to make anything from straight to curved lines.

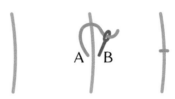

Place a single straight stitch. Bring your needle up through the fabric on one side of your previously laid stitch (A). Take your needle over to the other side of the laid thread and go down through the fabric (B). This will "pin" your stitch in place. You can do this as many or few times as you need to create your desired shape.

SATIN STITCH

Satin stitch is the fastest way to fill large areas in a design, like flower petals or leaves. It lays several stitches beside each other to create a solid and smooth block of color.

Traditionally, a satin stitch begins on one end of the shape you're filling and you work your way to the other end, but I actually prefer to start in the center. I fill one side and then go back to the middle to fill the opposite side. I find this method makes it easier to ensure symmetrical stitching. (If you stitch one side a little wonky, you can mirror it on the other side, which results in a more even shape.) As a bonus, you get the immediate satisfaction of finishing an area quicker.

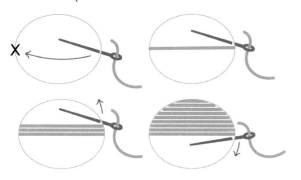

Place your first stitch along the center line of the shape you're filling by bringing the needle up from the back of your fabric, and then back down through the fabric at the opposite end of the shape (X).

Pull up the next stitch right beside your first stitch, and down at the opposite end of the shape again. The closer together your stitches li, the smoother the end result.

Repeat the process until one side of the shape is filled. Once the first side of the shape is filled, go back to the center and fill the other side.

Depending on the type of shape you're filling, you may need to create some diagonal stitches that overlap and share holes. This technique organically follows the shape you're stitching while keeping your satin stitch looking smooth. Here's an example.

Make a center line stitch as with the oval. Pull your needle up through the fabric right beside your previously placed stitch. Then bring it down through the same exit point as your previous stitch, resulting in an angled line that follows the outer shape of the petal.

If you continuously put your needle through the same hole, the base of the petal may become bulky. Combat this by occasionally placing a short diagonal stitch, which you can tuck under your last stitch.

You'll want to pull your needle through the fabric beside your last stitch. Then, instead of bringing your needle all the way to the base, simply tuck it under your last stitch about half way down the petal. Then you can continue stitching normally.

Note: When satin stitching on garments, the longer your stitches, the less neat they will look—especially after wearing and washing the garment. Long satin stitches also tend to snag. (I've pulled on stitches with my wedding ring more times than I can count.) This is why I almost always embellish my petals and leaves with some straight stitches, as a way to anchor the satin stitches down. You can also combat any pulling by adhering permanent interfacing to the back.

LEAF SATIN STITCH

Most often, embroiderers use a stitch called leaf stitch (or fishbone stitch) to fill in leaves. It's a technique where you place small stitches going back and forth between the sides of a leaf to fill it in. My approach is a bit different. I prefer to fill in one side of the leaf first, and then the other side. It creates a similar outcome, but I find it's faster and more intuitive to stitch a leaf this way.

This stitch is technically a satin stitch, but the placement of stitches is unique. Plus, leaves are used so often in this book that they deserve their own instruction!

Begin your leaf by placing a single stitch along the center; this line will act as a guide while you fill in the leaf and will help keep your stitches clean and even.

Pull up your needle at the top of the leaf, right beside your first stitch. Make a diagonal stitch that meets the center line, roughly half way down the leaf, and bring your needle down through the fabric.

Repeat the process, progressing down the center line until you meet the bottom of the leaf. When one side is filled, switch to the opposite side and do the same, starting at the top of the leaf and progressing all the way to the bottom.

LONG AND SHORT STITCH

If you're stitching an area that's too large for a satin stitch, a long and short stitch (occasionally called a brick stitch) is a great alternative. Long and short stitch is applied by embroidering rows of stitches in a varying size, which creates a brick-like effect. The main advantage to a long and short stitch is that it offers many contact points with the fabric, so you don't have to worry about threads getting pulled or coming undone—a necessity for garments that will see a lot of wear. It's common to use multiple colors for this technique, which is how "thread painting" is done. My preference is to use one color as a shape filler.

Traditionally, when embroidering with long and short stitch, the stitches are placed in adjoining rows where the stitches vary in length. I personally find it more intuitive to work the shape like a satin stitch, but instead of using long stitches that cover the entire surface, I create backstitches in single lines placed beside each other. Starting at the edge of your design, backstitch a line across the shape you are filling.

Starting once again at the edge, come up right beside your line of laid stitches and place another backstitch line, this time making the stitches shorter.

Repeat the process, alternating the length of stitches on each line. This technique is very forgiving; you can angle your stitches and even place stitches directly on top of each other.

Note: If you find your long and short stitches are looking too brick-like, vary the length of your stitches even more.

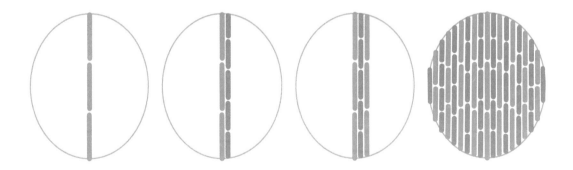

FRENCH KNOTS

French knots are small knots that are used like dots to fill in the inside of flowers, or as accents. Some people even stitch entire designs with nothing but French knots! The size of a French knot depends on the number of times you wrap your floss around the needle. Wrap once for a small knot, and many times for a large knot. (I usually wrap twice.)

When I'm teaching beginner embroidery classes, I save French knots for last. People new to the craft tend to be intimidated by them, but once you get the hang of them, they are a breeze!

Bring your needle up through the fabric where you want to place the knot, and pull the thread all the way through. Hold the needle in your dominant hand, and in your non-dominant hand, pinch the floss near the bottom of the strand (about an inch or two away from the fabric).

Angle the needle down, close to where you want to create your knot. With your non-

dominant hand, wrap the floss around the needle (away from yourself) once or twice, depending on your desired size of knot.

While holding the thread taut in your non stitching hand, push the needle back through the fabric right beside where you originally pulled up the thread.

Pull the needle and thread all the way through and you should be left with a cute little knot.

DETACHED CHAIN STITCH

A detached chain stitch (commonly called a lazy daisy stitch) is a standalone stitch used to create small petals or leafy accents. For the purpose of this guide, let's say we're stitching a petal.

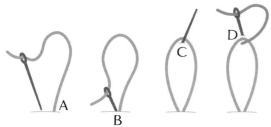

Start your stitch at the base of the petal by pulling your floss up all the way through the fabric (A). Bring the needle down through the fabric beside the hole you came out of (B). Don't pull the thread completely through, as a loop of floss is needed to create the proper shape of this stitch.

At the top of your petal, bring your needle through the inside of the loop (C) and pull the floss all the way through the fabric.

Secure the petal by bringing your needle down through the fabric, directly above the loop (D). Voilà!

CHAIN STITCH

A chain stitch is exactly what it sounds like: an embroidery stitch that looks like a chain. Chain stitch is traditionally used for linework, but these days many people use it to fill shapes. The technique is simple once you've mastered detached chain stitches, because you're basically making single loops continuously.

At your chosen starting point, place a loop (as if you were making a detached chain stitch) but don't pin the top. Bring your needle through the fabric in the center of the laid thread so you can create another loop.

Make the loop by bringing your needle back through the fabric. Continue this process as you work along your pattern.

When you're ready to end the chain stitch, simply secure the final loop by securing the top of the chain with a small tacking stitch.

notes on mending

Embroidery is a fantastic way to take your visible mending to the next level. Of course, embroidery with mending isn't a new thing. *Sashiko* is a Japanese technique of visible mending with embroidery that has been practiced for centuries. And any child of the eighties and nineties can tell you about their childhood jeans, mended with bold and brightly colored embroidered patches.

If you have a garment you would like to mend, you must first assess what type of mending is best for the situation. Sometimes a small nick or hole can simply be sewn shut, and an embroidered motif can be stitched right over the repair. If you have a large hole, you can sew the edges to prevent fraying, and then embroider a design on some fabric and attach the embroidered design as a patch right on top of the repair. If the design is larger than the patch, stitch directly over both the patch and the garment. Alternatively, if your design is smaller than the patch, you can stitch directly onto the fabric that will become the patch before attaching it.

To be completely honest, I'm not an expert on mending, and I wouldn't say I'm even particularly skilled at sewing. But I can fix the occasional hole in my family's clothing *and* make it look cute, so no one is complaining. I usually mend using embroidery floss instead of sewing thread, because I have lots of floss and I'm comfortable using it. And I'll use simple stitches like a running stitch or whipstitch (my personal favorite) that I illustrate on page 59. Mainly, I try to have fun with it. Using your imagination and creativity, you can take the designs featured in this book to adorn your old stitched-up clothes. Mending jeans is boring. Mending jeans while adding some embroidered plants? That is fun!

RUNNING STITCH

A running stitch is the most basic stitch in hand-sewing, and it is used prominently in *sashiko* mending. Quick and easy, it can be used for seams, creating shapes for visible mending, or to attach patches to worn areas.

A ——— B

Bring your needle through the fabric from back to front where you want to start your first stitch (A), and down through the fabric where you want to end the stitch (B).

C ——— D

Leaving a bit of space from the end of your last stitch, bring your needle up to start your next stitch (C), and then back down one stitch-length away (D). Try to keep the length of your stitches and gaps between consistent. This will result in a neater running stitch.

Continue placing stitches, moving up and down through the fabric, to create whatever shape you prefer.

WHIPSTITCH

Whipstitch is my go-to for mending because it's a secure way to close small holes, keep edges from fraying or ripping further, or attach a patch. It works especially well in mending the knees of jeans.

Mending a small hole

If the edges of a ripped garment can still touch, the hole is small enough to be sewn shut. Bring your needle through the fabric, back to front, one centimeter above the upper edge of the hole (A). Then, one centimeter below the lower edge of the hole, push your needle back through the fabric (B). As you pull the floss through the fabric, the hole will close in the spot you laid your thread.

Place the next stitch by bringing your needle through the fabric beside your previously laid stitch (A), approximately half a centimeter over in the direction you're stitching. Just as you did with the previous stitch, bring your needle through the fabric a centimeter below the hole and pull the floss to bring the two edges together (B).

Continue stitching to close the hole. To finish, simply tie a knot at the back of the fabric.

Preventing frayed edges

Approximately one centimeter from a ripped edge (illustrated in gray), bring your

needle through the fabric, from back to front (A). Move your needle under the edge of the fabric and bring your needle back through the fabric beside your previously laid stitch, approximately half a centimeter over in the direction you're stitching (B). Draw the floss all the way through. This should create a loop around the edge (C).

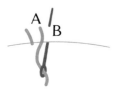

Using the same technique, move your needle under the fabric edge and then back up, half a centimeter over in the direction you're stitching.

Continue stitching along the edge of your fabric. To finish, tie a knot at the back of the fabric.

Adding a patch

Place the patch over the area you wish to cover. Starting on the upper portion of the patch, bring your needle through the

garment fabric, back to front, just above the top edge of the patch (A). Push your needle through the patch fabric, about a centimeter below the spot you brought the needle out (B). Then, come back up through the garment fabric approximately half a centimeter over in the direction you're stitching (C) and pull your thread all the way through to tighten the stitch.

Place the next stitch by bringing your needle through the patch fabric, about a centimeter below the spot you brought your needle out. Push the needle through the garment fabric, back to front, half a centimeter over in the direction you're working. Pull the thread all the way through to tighten the stitch.

Working clockwise, continue to stitch around the patch until you reach the point you started. To finish, tie a knot in the back of the garment fabric.

The projects

plain cotton tee, two ways 63

celestial cardigan 67

cacti ball cap 71

floral sweater 75

wildflower skirt 79

flourishing jean jacket 83

witchy dress 87

woodland sneakers 91

houseplant jean patch 95

market bag 99

crystal blazer 103

gardener's apron 107

blackwork-inspired tunic 111

folky moth camisole 115

harvest bandana 119

greenhouse backpack 123

four collars for four seasons 127

romantic rose bralette 133

plain cotton tee, two ways

A cotton T-shirt is one of the simplest garments to stitch on, with the added bonus that it's likely you already have a few folded in your drawer. If you've never picked up an embroidery needle or simply need a refresher, the floral motifs given here are a great way to learn and practice the most common stitches you'll find in the coming projects. This design is presented in two ways: one pattern with plain florals, and one with a snake woven throughout. The instructions are the same for both, with an additional step for the snake.

Materials

- Plain cotton T-shirt
- Transfer tools
- 5-inch (13 cm) embroidery hoop (if garment thickness allows)
- Backing stabilizer (optional)
- DMC embroidery floss
- Embroidery needle
- Embroidery scissors
- Soft-touch interfacing (optional)

Color Guide

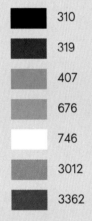

■	310
■	319
■	407
■	676
□	746
■	3012
■	3362

Pattern

Page 136

Instructions

1. Transfer the pattern to your shirt.
2. Hoop your pattern, or stabilize the fabric if necessary.
3. Begin your pattern by filling in the white petals with satin stitch.
4. Next, you'll want to add your accent color to your flowers to give them some dimension. Add the pink floss right on top of the satin stitched petals using straight stitches: I started my stitches roughly halfway up the petal and ended them at the bottom.
5. *Snake Option:* When stitching the flowers around the snake, I chose to keep them plain white. You can do the same, or add the accent color.
6. Fill the center of the flowers by placing a few French knots.
7. Next, fill in the leaves using a leaf satin stitch, and use a backstitch for the main stem and any stems attached to the leaves.
8. Once the leaves are filled, place a single straight stitch in the center of each leaf as an accent color. I started my stitch three-fourths of the way up from the bottom of the leaf and ended the stitch at the bottom.
9. Now you can move on to the dark green leafy accents. Place detached chain stitches (lazy daisy), and then add a backstitch for the stems.
10. *Snake Option*: Create the snake by backstitching along his outlines. You'll need to place your stitches closer together as you bend around tight curves.
11. Remove your hoop and any stabilizers and add soft-touch interfacing to the back of the embroidery (optional).

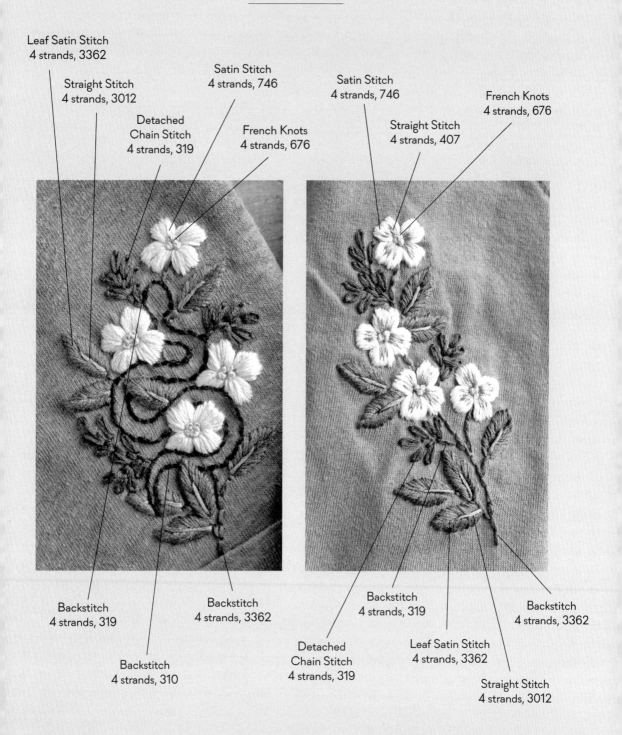

Leaf Satin Stitch
4 strands, 3362

Straight Stitch
4 strands, 3012

Detached
Chain Stitch
4 strands, 319

Satin Stitch
4 strands, 746

French Knots
4 strands, 676

Satin Stitch
4 strands, 746

Straight Stitch
4 strands, 407

French Knots
4 strands, 676

Backstitch
4 strands, 319

Backstitch
4 strands, 3362

Backstitch
4 strands, 310

Detached
Chain Stitch
4 strands, 319

Backstitch
4 strands, 319

Leaf Satin Stitch
4 strands, 3362

Backstitch
4 strands, 3362

Straight Stitch
4 strands, 3012

celestial cardigan

If you're looking for a quick project or a motif to reinforce snagged and unraveled knitwear, these little celestial designs are for you! I chose to add the designs to the pocket and breast of a knitted cardigan, but they could easily be applied to a winter hat, the ends of a knitted scarf, or a pair of mittens.

Materials

- Knitted cardigan
- Transfer tools
- 5-inch (13 cm) embroidery hoop (if garment thickness allows)
- Backing stabilizer (optional)
- DMC tapestry wool
- Chenille needle
- Needle threader
- Embroidery scissors
- Soft-touch interfacing (optional)

Color Guide

ecru

Pattern

Page 137

Instructions

1. Transfer the designs to your cardigan.
2. Hoop your pattern, or stabilize the fabric if necessary. My cardigan was too thick to hoop, so I used a backing stabilizer.
3. *The Sun*: Begin stitching the sun by filling the petals with a satin stitch. The space is quite tight, so you'll be able to fill each petal with only a few stitches.
4. Next, stitch the leaves by placing a leaf satin stitch. Then backstitch the stems and bases of the flower heads.
5. Using a stem stitch, work your way around the circle of the sun.
6. Finish the sun by backstitching the geometric lies on the outside.
7. *The Moon*: Fill the leaves using a leaf satin stitch, and backstitch any stems to connect the leaves together.
8. Place a stem stitch around the crescent shape of the moon, and backstitch the geometric lines.
9. Remove any stabilizers and add soft-touch interfacing to the back of the embroidery (optional).

Leaf Satin Stitch

Backstitch

Stem Stitch

Backstitch

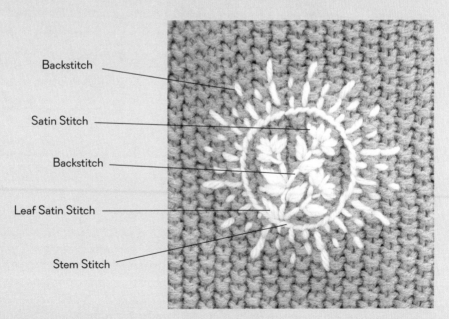

Backstitch

Satin Stitch

Backstitch

Leaf Satin Stitch

Stem Stitch

cacti
ball cap

If you want to play with textures in your embroidery, look no further than this friendly little cacti trio. I chose six strands of floss for my hat, but if your outerwear sees a lot of wear and will be washed and handled often, opt for four strands.

Materials

- Ball cap
- Transfer tools
- 4-inch (10 cm) embroidery hoop (if cap thickness allows)
- Backing stabilizer (optional)
- DMC embroidery floss
- Embroidery needle
- Embroidery scissors
- Soft-touch interfacing (optional)

Color Guide

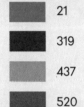

	21
	319
	437
	520
	730
	738
	3363

Pattern

Page 138

Instructions

1. Transfer the pattern to your hat.
2. Hoop your pattern, or stabilize the fabric if necessary.
3. Using a satin stitch, begin your pattern by filling in the tall cactus in the middle. Place your stitches horizontally, starting at the top and working your way to the bottom.
4. After the tall cactus is filled, take the darkest shade of brown floss and place French knots randomly all over the cactus. Use four strands of floss for these little accents.
5. Moving on to the two-toned cactus on the left, satin stitch one side with the dark shade of green, and then satin stitch the other side with a lighter shade. It's easiest to begin each stitch on the outside of the cactus, and end it in the center line.
6. Create the prickles by using four strands of floss in the medium brown color. Place small straight stitches randomly all over the cactus. I alternated between using single stitches, and two stitches to create a V shape.
7. To embroider the final cactus, use a satin stitch, placed horizontally, in all three sections of the cactus. It's easiest to fill the middle section first, and then the outer sections.
8. Using four strands of the pink floss, place small straight stitches at the top of the round cactus.
9. Finally, freehand some small X's with the palest shade of brown floss on top of the lines between the sections. Start by placing one small diagonal stitch, starting in one section and ending in the other. Then place another diagonal stitch facing the opposite way to complete your X.
10. Remove your hoop and any stabilizers.
11. Add soft-touch interfacing to the back of the embroidery (optional).

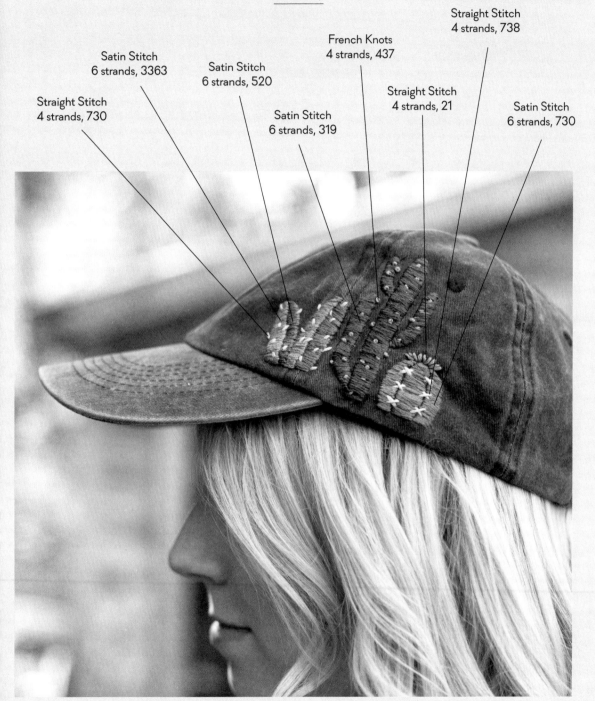

Straight Stitch
4 strands, 730

Satin Stitch
6 strands, 3363

Satin Stitch
6 strands, 520

Satin Stitch
6 strands, 319

French Knots
4 strands, 437

Straight Stitch
4 strands, 21

Straight Stitch
4 strands, 738

Satin Stitch
6 strands, 730

floral sweater

If you've never stitched on a sweater before, this simple floral project is a great place to start. You can embroider all the flowers, or split them up if you want a quicker project. Additionally, these flowers would be perfectly placed on the back pocket of denim jeans (using cotton floss), or along the sleeve of a sweater.

Tip: Depending on the size of your garment you can adjust the space between flowers, or use more or fewer of them to better match the width of your sweater.

Materials

- Sweater
- Dissolvable stabilizer
- Backing stabilizer (optional)
- 4- to 5-inch (10 to 13 cm) embroidery hoop (if garment thickness allows)
- DMC tapestry wool
- Chenille needle
- Needle threader
- Embroidery scissors
- Soft-touch interfacing (optional)

Color Guide

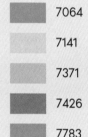

7064

7141

7371

7426

7783

7890

Pattern

Page 139

Instructions

1. Transfer the floral pattern to your sweater using a dissolvable stabilizer.
2. Stabilize the garment if required, and hoop your sweater if thickness allows.
3. Begin your flower by filling in the petals with a satin stitch. It's easiest to start at the outer edges of the petal and bring your stitches in to the center. Because the petals narrow in the center, you'll have to make a few diagonal stitches that overlap when they reach the center.
4. Fill in the large leaves next, using a leaf satin stitch.
5. You can add an accent to the leaves by placing two diagonal straight stitches: Start each stitch three-fourths of the way up the leaf, and end your stitch at the bottom of the leaf.
6. Fill in the small leaves with a leaf satin stitch, and backstitch any stems.
7. Stitch the small pink accent using a satin stitch. You'll only be able to fit a few stitches in the small area. Then stitch the branches with a backstitch.
8. Finish your flower by placing some French knots in the center.
9. Remove any stabilizers, and add soft-touch interfacing to the back of the embroidery (optional).

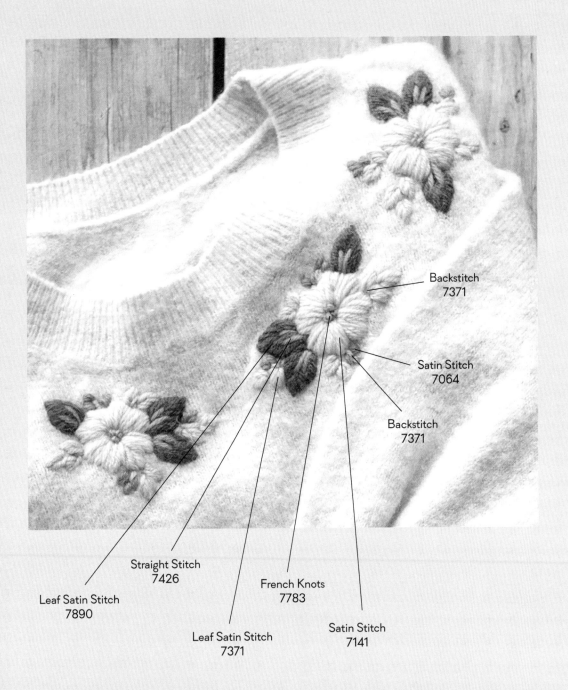

Backstitch
7371

Satin Stitch
7064

Backstitch
7371

Straight Stitch
7426

French Knots
7783

Leaf Satin Stitch
7890

Leaf Satin Stitch
7371

Satin Stitch
7141

wildflower skirt

I'm jealous of my daughter's closet. If you're wondering about her age, she's two. Most of her clothes feature dainty machine-embroidered florals, and fabrics printed with wildflowers and other charming motifs that clothing companies rarely offer to thirty-something adults like me. This embroidered wildflower skirt is the grown-up version of my daughter's clothing, inspired by the violets and tansy that grow wild in my city's beautiful river valley.

Materials

- Linen skirt
- Dissolvable stabilizer
- Backing stabilizer (optional)
- 5-inch (13 cm) embroidery hoop (if garment thickness allows)
- DMC embroidery floss
- Embroidery needle
- Embroidery scissors
- Soft-touch interfacing (optional)

Color Guide

 06

520

 783

935

 3012

 3052

Pattern

Page 140

Instructions

1. Transfer the patterns to your skirt by placing the motifs randomly on the garment. Try to space the motifs as evenly as possible. (Keep in mind, the closer together, the more stitching you'll have to do.) I randomly placed the motifs on the skirt, even placing some upside down and sideways.

2. Stabilize the garment if required, and hoop your skirt if thickness allows.

3. Start your skirt by stitching the violets: Begin the flowers by filling in the petals with a satin stitch. As the center of the violet is narrow, you'll have to make a few diagonal stitches that overlap when they reach the center.

4. Fill in the violet leaves using a leaf satin stitch. You'll notice the top of the leaves curve in to create a heart shape: To create this shape, simply angle your stitches into the center as you work your way to the bottom (tip) of the leaf. When the leaves are complete, stitch the stems by placing a backstitch along the lines on your pattern.

5. Moving onto the tansy, place horizontal satin stitches on each of the ovals to make the flower head.

6. Stitch the tansy stems by placing a backstitch and place a single stitch on every section of the fern-like leaves.

7. Finally, create the leafy branches with a leaf satin stitch. As the leaves are two-toned, stitch one side with one shade of green, and then the opposite side with another. Finish the branch with a backstitch on the stems to join the leaves together.

8. Remove your hoop and any stabilizers, and add soft-touch interfacing to the back of the embroidery (optional).

Backstitch
4 strands, 520

Satin Stitch
4 strands, 06

Leaf Satin Stitch
4 strands, 520

Satin Stitch
4 strands, 783

Backstitch
4 strands, 935

Backstitch
4 strands, 3012

Leaf Satin Stitch
4 strands, 3012

Leaf Satin Stitch
4 strands, 3052

flourishing jean jacket

The calligraphy on this jacket was designed by my talented friend Amelia, who calligraphs for a living. I took her lovely design and altered it ever so slightly to convert it to an embroidery pattern. I chose a jean jacket because they are thick and don't usually have much stretch, which makes them a perfect garment for embroidery with the added bonus that they can stand up to large designs and a full six strands of embroidery floss. The main thing to consider when working on a jean jacket is the placement of your pattern, as the bulky seams are nearly impossible to push a needle through. The top of this jacket was a blank canvas, making it the ideal spot to place the design, but I did have to cut out the interior label, as the thick leather would have gotten in the way of my stitches.

Materials

- Jean jacket
- Transfer tools
- 5-inch (13 cm) embroidery hoop (if garment thickness allows
- Backing stabilizer (optional)
- DMC embroidery floss
- Embroidery needle
- Embroidery scissors
- Soft-touch interfacing (optional)

Color Guide

B5200

Pattern

Page 141

Instructions

1. Transfer the pattern to your jean jacket.
2. Hoop or stabilize the fabric. As you work, you'll need to move the hoop around the design.
3. Start stitching the wording by placing a backstitch along the thin lines, in the same direction you would write, working from left to right. Try to keep the length of your stitches as even as possible. (But you'll need to make them smaller when stitching around tight curves.)
4. To fill the thick areas, use a long and short stitch. Start the long and short stitch by outlining the letters with a backstitch, and then fill the interiors with alternating lines until filled.
5. To dot the *i*'s, simply place vertical satin stitches.
6. Finish the lettering by filling the leaves with a leaf satin stitch.
7. Remove your hoop and any stabilizers, and add soft-touch interfacing to the back of the embroidery (optional).

Leaf Satin Stitch
6 strands

Long and Short Stitch
6 strands

Backstitch
6 strands

Satin Stitch
6 strands

witchy dress

I have a bit of an obsession with witches. Give me a witch-focused television show or book, and you'll have a happy Alex. I'm drawn to witches because they have been the ultimate feminists throughout history, and I love how today's modern style is seeing a resurgence in witchy aesthetics. This design is my ode to modern witches.

The pattern for this dress is split into two sections, so you can adjust the design to your liking. I chose to stitch the design as one large statement piece on my dress, but you can divide the design into halves and place them separately on your clothing.

Note: The pattern was larger than my hoop. I moved the hoop around and placed it right on top of the laid embroidery. It's fine to do this, but try to not keep the hoop on for too long. If you're taking a break from stitching, remove the hoop and re-hoop when you're ready to start again. This will prevent indents in your stitchwork.

Materials

- Black dress
- Transfer tools
- Backing stabilizer (optional)
- 7-inch (18 cm) embroidery hoop (if garment allows)
- DMC embroidery floss
- Embroidery needle
- Embroidery scissors
- Soft-touch interfacing (optional)

Color Guide

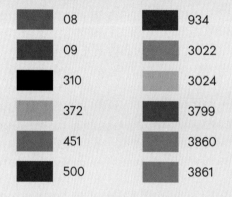

08	934
09	3022
310	3024
372	3799
451	3860
500	3861

Pattern

Pages 142–143

Instructions

1. Place the pattern on your garment and stabilize the fabric if necessary.
2. Fill in the petals of the large purple flowers with a satin stitch. It's easiest to start at the outer edges of the petal and bring your stitches in to the center.
3. Next, add the accent color to your large flowers. The pale flower in the middle uses the same purple you previously used to stitch the darker flowers, and the remaining flowers use a lighter shade of purple. Add the floss right on top of the satin stitched petals using straight stitches: I started my stitches roughly halfway up the petal, and ended them at the center.
4. To finish the large flowers, you'll need to fill the centers. Using a light shade of grey, place a satin stitch to fill the middle circle. Next, take some black embroidery floss and place a ring of French knots between the circle and petals.
5. Once the flowers are complete, fill the green foliage using a leaf satin stitch, and the stems using a backstitch.
6. Finish off this section of flowers by stitching the small branchy accent florals. Begin by filling in the petals with a satin stitch and placing a single French knot in the center of the flowers. Next, take your brown floss and satin stitch the base of the budding petals. Using the same color, backstitch the branches.
7. Use a satin stitch for the lily of the valley. Start at the bottom of the flowers and end your stitches at the top. As you stitch your way to the outer edges, angle the stitches into the top (center) of the flowers—this will create a nice bell shape.
8. The next step is to fill the two-toned leaves using a leaf satin stitch. Creating a two-toned leaf isn't much different from a plain leaf. You'll notice the leaf has a line down the middle; this line separates

Leaf Satin Stitch
6 strands, 3022

Leaf Satin Stitch
6 strands, 500

Backstitch or
Couching
6 strands, 372

French Knots
6 strands, 372

Leaf Satin Stitch
6 strands, 934

Backstitch
6 strands, 934

Satin Stitch
6 strands, 310

French Knots
6 strands, 3799

Satin Stitch
6 strands, 09

Satin Stitch
6 strands, 451

Satin Stitch
6 strands, 3024

Backstitch
6 strands, 08

Satin Stitch
6 strands, 3861

Satin Stitch
6 strands, 3024

Satin Stitch
6 strands, 09

Satin Stitch
6 strands, 3860

the colors and will act as your guide as you fill in your leaf. Start at the top of your leaf and make a diagonal stitch meeting your center line. Repeat the process on one side, progressing down your line until you meet the bottom of the leaf. Then switch to the opposite side and do the same with your other color.

9. After you fill the lily of the valley leaves, take the dark green floss you just used and place a stem stitch on each of the lines to create the stems.

10. Using the same floss color used for the lily of the valley flowers, fill the moon with a satin stitch. I found it easiest to start at one corner of the moon and work my way to the other corner.

11. The last bit of stitching you'll have to do on this design is the magical stars. As they are quite small, you may prefer to use four strands of floss. (I used the full six.) I couched each section of the star, but you may find it easiest to use a backstitch. If couching, make a straight stitch between each point on the star, and place an anchoring stitch in the middle of the laid thread to create a curved line.

12. Remove your hoop and add soft-touch interfacing to the back of the embroidery (optional).

woodland sneakers

I put off embroidering on shoes for a long time, as I was nervous it would be difficult. Turns out, stitching on shoes is actually pretty simple! After some trial and error, I've come up with two rules for stitching on sneakers: First, they must be made from a fabric you can pierce a needle through without too much resistance (like canvas). It's worth noting that sneakers made of even the thinnest fabrics can be tough to get a needle through, so I highly recommend using a thimble. Second is to consider the placement of your pattern. Ideally, choose a spot with no seams, as it's almost impossible to stitch over a seam on a shoe. Another important consideration is that you must to be able to get your hand inside the shoe where your pattern is. If your hand doesn't fit you won't be able to bring your needle through the fabric from the inside.

Now that we have the basics out of the way, you can start stitching! I designed this pattern so you can experiment with the placement of the individual woodland motifs to create your own designs. This will allow you to embroider on different types of shoes, ranging from slip-ons to high-tops!

Materials

- Canvas shoes
- Dissolvable stabilizer
- DMC embroidery floss
- Embroidery needle
- Embroidery scissors
- Thimble (optional)

Color Guide

■	08	■	842
■	347	■	895
■	524	■	898
■	712	■	937
■	739	■	3790

Pattern

Page 144

Instructions

1. Begin this project by removing any laces that may get in the way, then transfer the patterns to your shoes. Dissolvable stabilizer works well for shoes because you can move the motifs around while figuring out the perfect placement.
2. Fill in the mushrooms: Start by placing a satin stitch, horizontally, to fill the mushroom cap.
3. Once the cap is stitched, take some white floss and place a few straight stitches in random spots on the cap. You can make the spots more visually interesting by varying the size of each spot. To create larger spots, simply lay two straight stitches right beside each other.
4. Finish the mushroom by filling the stalk with a satin stitch, placed vertically.
5. Stich the acorns by filling the nut (bottom) with a satin stitch, placed vertically. It's easiest to start each stitch at the top of the nut and end at the bottom.
6. Next, take a darker shade of brown and fill in the top of the acorn by placing a horizontal satin stitch.
7. Complete the acorn by placing a vertical satin stitch to fill the stems.
8. Moving on to the small brown branches, place a backstitch to create the branches. Once the branches have been stitched, take your cream-colored floss and place French knots on the end of each branch.
9. Next, the long leafy branches: Fill in the leaves using a leaf satin stitch, and backstitch the stems using the same color.
10. Create the buds on the end of each branch by placing a satin stitch on each circle, using a light pink floss.
11. Finally, move on to the single leaves. Place a leaf satin stitch and fill in the leaf.

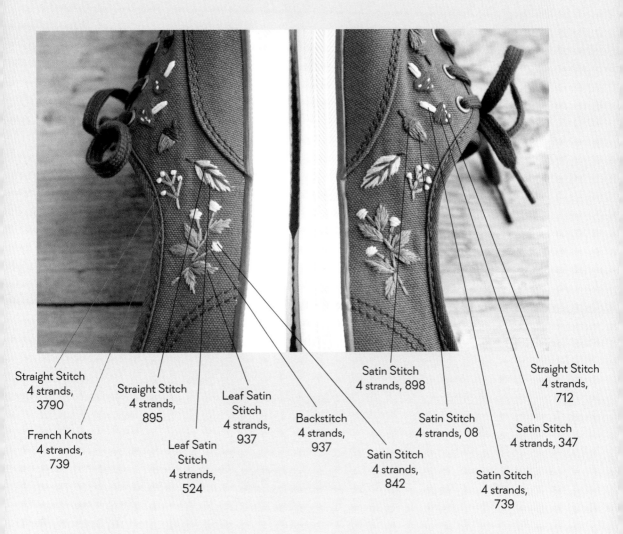

Straight Stitch
4 strands,
3790

French Knots
4 strands,
739

Straight Stitch
4 strands,
895

Leaf Satin
Stitch
4 strands,
524

Leaf Satin
Stitch
4 strands,
937

Backstitch
4 strands,
937

Satin Stitch
4 strands,
842

Satin Stitch
4 strands, 898

Satin Stitch
4 strands, 08

Satin Stitch
4 strands,
739

Straight Stitch
4 strands,
712

Satin Stitch
4 strands, 347

12. Once the leaf is filled, take an accent color and place a single straight stitch down the middle of the leaf, starting at the top and ending at the bottom. Then create veins by placing two angled straight stitches on each side of the leaf, starting at the outside of the leaf and angling your stitches to meet in the center line.

13. Finish the leaf by placing a final straight stitch under the leaf to create a stem.

14. Remove any stabilizers, re-lace your shoes, and take them for a stroll.

93

houseplant jean patch

I created this design as a fun way to mend a hole in a pair of jeans, but you don't have to use this design as a patch. You can easily split the houseplants into individual motifs, or stitch them as is on a back pocket.

If you're fixing a small hole, you can simply sew it shut and stitch directly on top—no need for a patch! The hole in my jeans was too large for a quick fix, so I sewed the edges of the rip to stop the hole from getting larger. I then took a second pair of worn-out jeans and stitched the potted plants onto a structurally sound area on the shin. Once I finished the embroidery, I cut a square around the houseplants; then I sewed the square onto the jeans.

Materials

- Jeans
- Transfer tools
- 5-inch (13 cm) embroidery hoop
- Backing stabilizer (optional)
- DMC embroidery floss
- Embroidery needle
- Embroidery scissors
- Soft-touch interfacing (optional)
- Sewing pins (optional)
- Material from excess fabric, if needed, to make a patch

Color Guide

■	310	■	904
■	319	■	975
■	433	■	988
■	435	■	3052
■	746		

Pattern

Page 145

Instructions

1. Place the pattern on your patch material and hoop or stabilize fabric if necessary.
2. Starting with the plant on the top left, fill in the rounded leaves with a leaf satin stitch, and use the same color to place a backstitch line for the stems.
3. Take your accent color and place a backstitch along the middle of the leaf, starting at the bottom of each leaf and ending at the tip. Then place two diagonal straight stitches on each side of the leaf, starting on the outer edges and ending in the middle line.
4. Fill the pot with a satin stitch, placed horizontally, carefully working around the previously laid leaves.
5. Finish the pot by freehanding some black lines directly on top of the satin stitch: Start by placing a backstitch, vertically, down the middle of the pot. Then add a couple backstitched lines on both sides. You should now have four lines stitched vertically down your pot. To add the horizontal lines you'll do the same, but place the backstitch horizontally: Start with the middle line and place a backstitch starting from the left side of the pot and ending at the right. Then add a horizontal line above and below.
6. Stitch the plant on the right by placing a leaf satin stitch on each of the leaves, and a backstitch along the branches.
7. Start the pot by placing a satin stitch on the upper triangles; it's easiest to start at the top of the pot and end the stitches at the bottoms. Since the points of the triangles are narrow, you'll have to angle some of your stitches and overlap them in the centers.
8. Using the same technique, take your darker floss color and fill the triangles on the bottom of the pot, this time starting at the bottom. Once the pot is filled, take the same darker color and fill the legs on the pot using a vertical satin stitch.

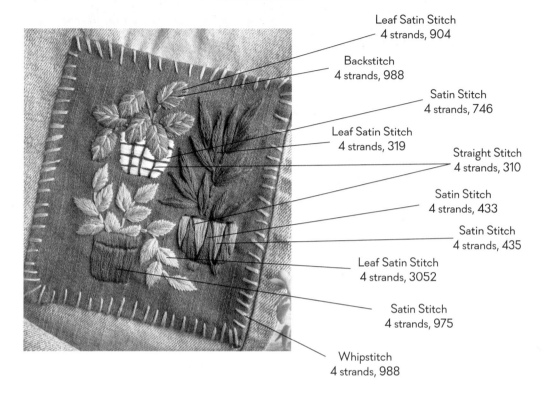

Leaf Satin Stitch
4 strands, 904

Backstitch
4 strands, 988

Satin Stitch
4 strands, 746

Leaf Satin Stitch
4 strands, 319

Straight Stitch
4 strands, 310

Satin Stitch
4 strands, 433

Satin Stitch
4 strands, 435

Leaf Satin Stitch
4 strands, 3052

Satin Stitch
4 strands, 975

Whipstitch
4 strands, 988

9. Complete the pot by placing a backstitch with some black floss along the top of the pot and in between the triangles. Use the outlines as an opportunity to clean the edges of any wonky stitchwork.

10. Begin stitching the final plant (lower left) by filling the leaves with a leaf satin stitch, and using a backstitch on the stems to join all the leaves on the vine.

11. Fill the pot with a satin stitch, placed vertically. Fill the top section first, and then the bottom.

12. Remove the hoop and any stabilizers, and add soft-touch interfacing to the back of the embroidery (optional).

To Sew on Your Patch

13. When you're finished embroidering, measure and mark a rectangular area around the embroidery and cut it out of the patch material.

14. Place the patch over the area you wish to mend, and fold in just enough of the the outside edges of the patch so the fabric doesn't unravel. You can pin the patch onto the garment with sewing pins. It's common to use an iron to flatten the outside edges after folding them in. I personally don't enjoy ironing, so I skip this step and live with imperfect edges.

15. Sew the patch onto the jeans with a whipstitch.

market bag

I have in my possession a cloth tote that was sewn by my grandma many decades ago. It's been well-loved and returned to my grandma many times for mending and reinforcements. She used thick wool and some type of felt-like fiber to embroider onions on the front. It's whimsical, and I adore it. My onion bag, as I call it, was the inspiration for this tote. Sure, there's only one onion in this design, but it has the playful spirit of the onion bag.

Materials

- Tote bag
- Transfer tools
- Backing stabilizer (optional)
- 6-inch (15 cm) embroidery hoop (if tote thickness allows)
- DMC tapestry wool
- Chenille needle
- Needle threader
- Embroidery scissors
- Soft-touch interfacing (optional)

Color Guide

 7624

Pattern

Pages 146–147

Instructions

1. Transfer the design to a tote bag.
2. Hoop your pattern, and stabilize the fabric if necessary.
3. With the exception of the strawberry seeds, which are single straight stitches, the entire pattern is embroidered with a backstitch. Start anywhere you would like and stitch along the lines of the pattern. The trick to keeping your lines neat is to make each stitch as similar in size as possible. When stitching long straight sections (like the onion leaves), it's tempting to use longer stitches, but try to keep them as even as possible.
4. Remove any stabilizers and add soft-touch interfacing to the back of the embroidery (optional).

Straight Stitch
7624

Backstitch
7624

crystal blazer

This design is for the people who love the power of crystals, or a power blazer. Since the crystals are placed near the edge of your garment, you won't be able to use a hoop. Luckily, many blazers are made of thick materials (polyester, wool) which can hold up without a backing stabilizer while you stitch. If your blazer is made of a thin fabric like cotton, you will need to use a backing to keep the fabric taut.

Because the crystal patterns are separated, you can place them however you like on your blazer. A dissolvable stabilizer works well for this type of pattern, as you can move the stickers around while you play with the placement of the designs.

You'll also notice there are no accent lines in the pattern. The lines are freehand because you'll use them to fill negative space, and every garment is unique. To create the lines, you'll be working with DMC's sparkly Light Effects floss, which can be challenging; my advice is to split the floss into fewer strands, and work with short sections of floss so it doesn't tangle on itself. You'll also likely need both a needle threader and a needle with a large eye. (Size 1 should do the trick.)

Materials

- Blazer
- Dissolvable stabilizer
- Backing stabilizer (optional)
- DMC embroidery floss
- Embroidery needle
- Embroidery scissors
- Soft-touch interfacing (optional)

Color Guide

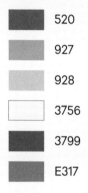

	520
	927
	928
	3756
	3799
	E317

Pattern

Page 147

Instructions

1. Place the pattern on your garment using a dissolvable stabilizer.
2. Stabilize fabric if necessary.
3. Fill each section of the crystals with satin stitch. There are three shades of blue, which I placed randomly through each section of the crystals. I also changed the direction of my satin stitches with each section. This keeps the crystals looking multidimensional.
4. Next, outline the crystals by placing a backstitch around each segment.
5. Take your green embroidery floss and fill in the leaves with a leaf satin stitch, and then place a backstitch to create the stems.
6. Finally, freehand straight stitches in rows to create the sparkly accents. It's best to work in sections and tie off each section of lines to keep the floss from unraveling.
7. Remove any stabilizers, and add soft-touch interfacing to the back of the embroidery (optional).

Satin Stitch
4 strands, 927

Satin Stitch
4 strands, 928

Satin Stitch
4 strands, 3756

Backstitch
4 strands, 3799

Leaf Satin Stitch
4 strands, 520

Backstitch
4 strands, 520

Straight Stitch
4 strands, E317

gardener's apron

This design is inspired by my love of gardening. During the summer I spend most of my spare time putzing around in my backyard, aimlessly weeding and pinching and deadheading. I chose an apron for this project because I'm consistently in need of larger pockets when I'm in the garden, and these pockets can hold a whole lot of tomatoes! If you're not an apron-wearing person, these designs would be lovely on some overalls.

Materials

- Apron
- Transfer tools
- Backing stabilizer (optional)
- 5-inch (13 cm) embroidery hoop (if garment allows)
- DMC embroidery floss
- Embroidery needle
- Embroidery scissors

Color Guide

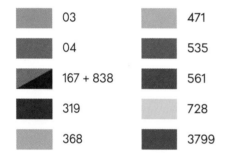

	03		471
	04		535
	167 + 838		561
	319		728
	368		3799

Pattern

Page 148

Instructions

1. Place the patterns on your apron, and hoop or stabilize the fabric (if necessary).
2. Begin the pattern by stitching the sunflower petals. Place two straight stitches tightly beside each other on each line.
3. To fill the sunflower centers, take both the light and dark brown floss and split each into three strands. Take three strands from the light brown and add it to the three strands of dark brown, to create a full six strands of two-toned floss. Thread your needle with the two-toned floss and fill the centers of the sunflowers with French knots.
4. Next, fill the sunflower leaves with a leaf satin stitch, and backstitch the stems with the same color.
5. Finish the leaves by placing a single straight stitch in the center of each leaf, using an accent color. Stitch three-fourths of the way up the leaf, and end your stitch at the bottom of the leaf.
6. Move on to the watering can; start by placing a satin stitch along the handle.
7. Next, fill the three sections in the middle with satin stitch, placed horizontally. After the sections are filled, take some gray floss that is one shade darker, and backstitch around each segment to outline the watering can.
8. Using the same (accent) color, fill in the long part of the spout with a satin stitch, and finally, take the same shade as the handle to fill in the top of the spout.
9. Start the scissors by filling in the handles with a satin stitch, placed horizontally. Then stitch the shears with another satin stitch, but this time place the stitches at an angle.
10. Stitch the spade by placing a horizontal satin stitch on the handle with a dark gray floss. Then place a satin stitch horizontally on the spade

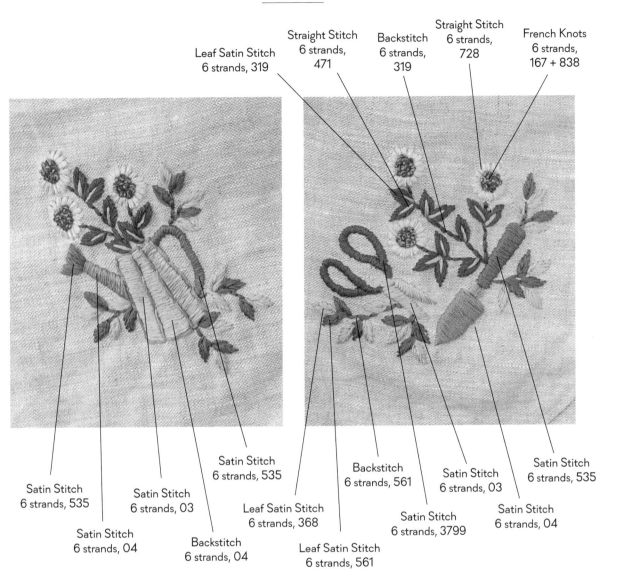

Leaf Satin Stitch
6 strands, 319

Straight Stitch
6 strands,
471

Backstitch
6 strands,
319

Straight Stitch
6 strands,
728

French Knots
6 strands,
167 + 838

Satin Stitch
6 strands, 535

Satin Stitch
6 strands, 535

Satin Stitch
6 strands, 03

Satin Stitch
6 strands, 535

Backstitch
6 strands, 561

Satin Stitch
6 strands, 03

Satin Stitch
6 strands, 04

Satin Stitch
6 strands, 04

Leaf Satin Stitch
6 strands, 368

Satin Stitch
6 strands, 3799

Backstitch
6 strands, 04

Leaf Satin Stitch
6 strands, 561

with a lighter gray. Finally, use the same lighter gray shade to fill in the joining area with a vertical satin stitch.

11. Fill in the accent leaves by placing a leaf satin stitch with alternating colors, and then backstitch with the darker shade to join the leaves together.

12. Remove the hoop and stabilizers, and add soft-touch interfacing to the back of the embroidery (optional).

blackwork-inspired tunic

Blackwork embroidery is a traditional technique where the stitcher uses a single thread color to place repeating geometric or floral designs inside a large shape. While historically the designs were created with dainty intricate stitches, this project uses modern shapes while taking inspiration from the use of repetition and floral details inside a larger design.

There are three patterns for this project, which can be laid out in an infinite number of combinations. When planning my own layout, I traced the designs onto plain paper and moved them around on my tunic until I was happy with the placement. I recommend doing the same before transferring the patterns to your garment.

Materials

- Tunic
- Transfer tools
- 5-inch (13 cm) embroidery hoop (if garment allows)
- Backing stabilizer (optional)
- DMC embroidery floss
- Embroidery needle
- Embroidery scissors
- Soft-touch interfacing (optional)

Color Guide

 310

Pattern

Page 149

Instructions

1. Decide on the layout of your patterns, and transfer them to your garment.
2. Hoop or stabilize the fabric if necessary.
3. Starting with the large diamond design, place a chain stitch along the diamond shape. It's easiest to begin at the top of the diamond and work your way around the shape clockwise.

4. Next, place a stem stitch along the scallops that connect with the diamond.
5. Fill in the accent petals on the corners of the diamond using a satin stitch. Once they are filled, if there's a gap between the petals and the chain stitched diamond, you can place a small straight stitch to connect them.
6. Moving on to the flower in the center, fill in the flower petals with a satin stitch and the leaves with a leaf satin stitch.
7. Finish the flower by placing a split stitch along the stems.
8. Once the large diamond design is complete, stitch the other motifs using the same stitches: satin stitch for the petals, leaf satin stitch for the leaves, and split stitch for all the stems and connecting lines.
9. Remove your hoop and add soft-touch interfacing to the back of the embroidery (optional).

Satin Stitch
6 strands

Chain Stitch
6 strands

Stem Stitch
6 strands

Satin Stitch
6 strands

Split Stitch
6 strands

Satin Stitch
6 strands

113

folky moth camisole

I used a long and short stitch to embroider the moths in this design. This is a stitch I don't usually use as a shape filler, opting instead for a satin stitch, but a long and short stitch offers an interesting texture and has more contact points with the fabric, which makes the moth designs work well for patching up a small hole on the shirt.

Note: I find long and short stitch can look busy, especially in a design with many details. Years ago, during my painting days, I was told by my artist mother-in-law that busy paintings need areas of calm for the eyes to rest. This is true of embroidery as well. To create areas of calm I like to mix long and short stitch with smoother stitches like satin stitch.

Materials

- Camisole or tank top
- Transfer tools
- 5-inch (13 cm) embroidery hoop (if garment allows)
- Backing stabilizer (optional)
- DMC embroidery floss
- Embroidery needle
- Embroidery scissors
- Soft-touch interfacing (optional)

Color Guide

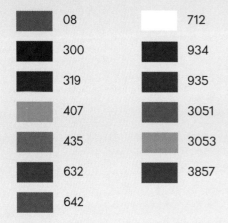

08	712
300	934
319	935
407	3051
435	3053
632	3857
642	

Pattern

Pages 150–151

Instructions

1. Transfer the patterns to your garment.
2. Hoop or stabilize the fabric.
3. Starting with the center moth, fill the outside of the wings with a satin stitch, placed horizontally, and do the same for the next section of the wing.

   In the center of the wing, fill in the orange accents with a satin stitch.

Then stitch the remaining area with a long and short stitch, starting at the outer edge and working your way to the middle of the moth.

The body of the center moth has three sections: Fill the head with a satin stitch, placed horizontally, and a backstitch for the antennae. Using the same color, stitch the bottom of the body with a long and short stitch, placed vertically. Finish the middle of the body by placing a horizontal satin stitch with a lighter accent color.

4. Begin the left moth by filling his body with a long and short stitch, placed vertically, and then a backstitch along the antennae.

   Use a satin stitch to create the moons on the upper wings, and another satin stitch to create the small circles along the edge of the inner wing.

   Place a horizontal long and short stitch on the inner wing, carefully stitching around the moon and circles you just laid. Then fill the outside of the upper wing using a vertical long and short stitch.

   Finish the left moth by filling his lower wings with a long and short stitch, placed horizontally.

5. Stitch the moth on the right, starting with the wings: Fill the pointy leaves with a leaf satin stitch, and then the rounded leaves on both the upper and lower wings with another leaf satin stitch.

   Fill the crescent shape of the moon with a satin stitch, placed vertically, and then a horizontal satin stitch for the circle underneath.

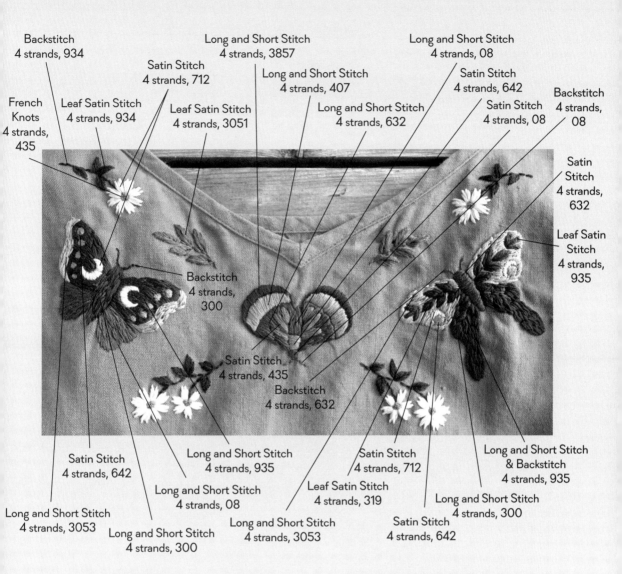

Backstitch
4 strands, 934

Long and Short Stitch
4 strands, 3857

Long and Short Stitch
4 strands, 08

Satin Stitch
4 strands, 712

Long and Short Stitch
4 strands, 407

Satin Stitch
4 strands, 642

French
Knots
4 strands,
435

Leaf Satin Stitch
4 strands, 934

Leaf Satin Stitch
4 strands, 3051

Long and Short Stitch
4 strands, 632

Satin Stitch
4 strands, 08

Backstitch
4 strands,
08

Satin
Stitch
4 strands,
632

Leaf Satin
Stitch
4 strands,
935

Backstitch
4 strands,
300

Satin Stitch
4 strands, 435

Backstitch
4 strands, 632

Satin Stitch
4 strands, 642

Long and Short Stitch
4 strands, 935

Long and Short Stitch
& Backstitch
4 strands, 935

Long and Short Stitch
4 strands, 08

Leaf Satin Stitch
4 strands, 319

Satin Stitch
4 strands, 712

Long and Short Stitch
4 strands, 300

Long and Short Stitch
4 strands, 3053

Long and Short Stitch
4 strands, 300

Long and Short Stitch
4 strands, 3053

Satin Stitch
4 strands, 642

Use a long and short stitch to fill both the upper and lower wings, carefully stitching around the leaves. Place your stitches horizontally for the upper wings, and vertically for the lower.

Finish the moth by filling the body with a satin stitch and backstitching the antennae.

6. Fill the flowers using a satin stitch for the petals, and French knots in the center.

7. Place a leaf satin stitch on each of the leaves, and backstitch the flower stems.

8. Stitch the rounded leaf motifs with a leaf satin stitch on each leaf and a backstitch on each stem.

9. Remove the embroidery hoop and add soft-touch interfacing to the back of the embroidery (optional).

harvest bandana

The photography for this book was done by Jenna Hobbs, who lives on a cute little farm and has an impeccable sense of style for someone who spends her days herding children and goats. During the first photoshoot for this book, she showed up wearing a rust-colored linen bandana, which I promptly asked to borrow for the purpose of stitching on. The design is inspired by her folky-farm style, and the project is fairly straightforward, as there are only a couple colors and stitches used. Additionally, the stitching is quite secure, so you can roll up your bandana to use it as a headband or decorative bow on a purse.

Materials

- Bandana
- Transfer tools
- 5-inch (13 cm) embroidery hoop
- Backing stabilizer (optional)
- DMC embroidery floss
- Embroidery needle
- Embroidery scissors
- Soft-touch interfacing (optional)

Color Guide

310

437

738

Pattern

Pages 152–153

Instructions

1. Transfer the pattern to your bandana. Placing the pattern on the bottom triangular area is ideal, as the top and sides of bandanas tend to not be visible when wrapped around a neck.
2. Hoop or stabilize the fabric.
3. Start by filling the sun with a satin stitch. While extending each stitch horizontally across each ray, work your way from the circle of the sun outward to the smallest point of the rays.
4. Move on to the wheat-colored leaves at the top left of the pattern. Embroider the leaves with a leaf satin stitch, and backstitch the branches to connect the leaves.
5. To embroider the flower in the top middle of the design, fill the petals with a satin stitch using black floss. Once the flower is filled, stitch the stem and leaves using a split stitch.
6. Begin the large flowers by filling the leaves with a leaf satin stitch, and then the stems with a stem stitch.
7. Stitch the flower heads using a backstitch, and then take your black floss and place 3 single straight stitches on top, and a French knot to finish the lines.
8. Remove any stabilizers, and add soft-touch interfacing to the back of the embroidery (optional).

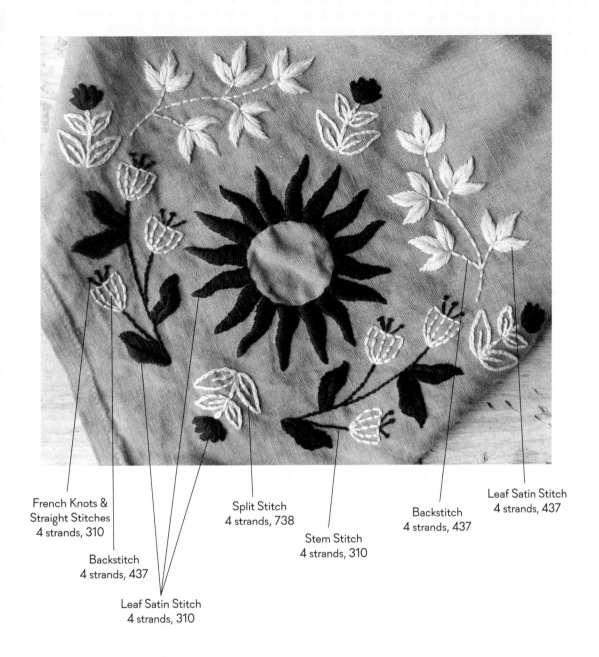

French Knots &
Straight Stitches
4 strands, 310

Backstitch
4 strands, 437

Leaf Satin Stitch
4 strands, 310

Split Stitch
4 strands, 738

Stem Stitch
4 strands, 310

Backstitch
4 strands, 437

Leaf Satin Stitch
4 strands, 437

greenhouse backpack

The backpack I used for this project is made by a popular brand, with a prominent logo stitched right in the middle of the bag. I thought it would be fun to cut off the logo and stitch something more appealing in its place. Much like canvas shoes, cotton or canvas backpacks are easy to stitch on. They have no stretch so you won't need a hoop, but you'll likely need a thimble as the fabric is usually thick. My backpack had a liner inside, which made it a challenge, because the two layers were quite resistant to the needle. It was doable, but I needed a thimble on both my thumb and middle finger to push the needle through the fabric.

I designed this little greenhouse to be the perfect size and shape to replace labels. If your bag has a stitched logo, try to cut it off before embroidering. If you aren't able to remove the label, you can transfer the pattern right over it and fill the negative space with some blue floss and a satin stitch. This will hide the logo nicely.

Materials

- Cotton or canvas backpack
- Transfer tools
- DMC embroidery floss
- Embroidery needle
- Embroidery scissors
- Soft-touch interfacing (optional)

Color Guide

 310

 505

 733

 890

935

3345

3346

Pattern

Page 151

Instructions

1. Remove the label if possible, and transfer the pattern to the bag.
2. Begin the pattern by backstitching the greenhouse outlines, placing long single stitches along each line and ending each stitch where they intersect. As you fill in the leaves, you'll have to work around the lines.
3. Fill the vining leaves at the top with a satin stitch. It's easiest to start your stitches at the leaf bottom (jagged edge) and end at the top. Once the leaves are complete, stitch the vines with a backstitch.
4. Move on to the leaves at the bottom left and top right corners: Fill them with a leaf satin stitch.
5. Next, stitch the two-toned leaves with a leaf satin stitch. Creating a two-toned leaf isn't much different from a plain leaf: You'll notice the leaf has a line down the middle; this line separates the colors and will act as your guide as you fill in your leaf. On one side of the leaf, start at the top and make a stitch meeting your center line. Repeat the process on one side, progressing down your line until you meet the bottom of the leaf. Then switch to the opposite side and do the same with your other color. Alternate the color placement on each leaf—this will keep them looking visually interesting. When both sides of the leaves are stitched, take your accent color and place a straight stitch in the middle of each leaf.
6. Once the two-toned leaves are complete, backstitch the branches using the dark green shade of floss.
7. Finally, fill the remaining leaves on the bottom right with a leaf satin stitch, and backstitch the branches with the same color.
8. Remove any stabilizers, and add soft-touch interfacing to the back of the embroidery (optional).

Backstitch
4 strands, 3345

Satin Stitch
4 strands, 3345

Backstitch
4 strands, 310

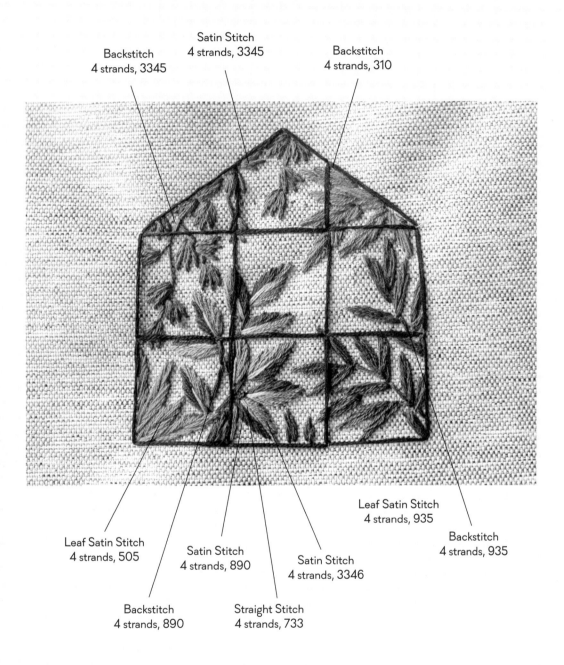

Leaf Satin Stitch
4 strands, 505

Satin Stitch
4 strands, 890

Leaf Satin Stitch
4 strands, 935

Satin Stitch
4 strands, 3346

Backstitch
4 strands, 935

Backstitch
4 strands, 890

Straight Stitch
4 strands, 733

four collars for four seasons

Everyone has a season they love the most. For me, it's a tie between summer and fall. I think seasonal preferences have something to do with where you live, or what your favorite holidays are. Whatever your favorite season is, you can rep it with a collared shirt, embroidered with fun seasonal motifs.

To transfer these patterns, consider using a dissolvable stabilizer if you have it on hand. It will allow you to effortlessly move the designs around on your collar while figuring out the perfect placement. If you have a collared shirt that looks different from the ones in the photo, don't worry! Playing with pattern placement will enable you to utilize the designs in a way that works for your own shirt.

Materials

- Collared shirt
- Transfer tools
- Backing stabilizer (optional)
- DMC embroidery floss
- Embroidery needle
- Embroidery scissors
- Soft-touch interfacing (optional)

Color Guide

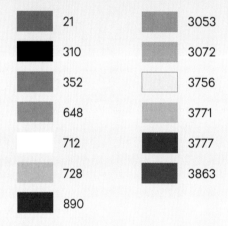

21	3053
310	3072
352	3756
648	3771
712	3777
728	3863
890	

Pattern

Pages 153–154

Instructions

Spring

1. Transfer the pattern to your collar and stabilize if necessary.
2. Embroider the ladybug by first filling the black spots with satin stitch. Then fill both the head and area under the wings with a satin stitch. Place a single straight stitch between the wings, and finish with your black thread by backstitching the antennae and legs. When the black areas are complete, take your red floss and carefully satin stitch around the spots to fill the wings.
3. Fill the leaves with a leaf satin stitch, and backstitch the stems.
4. Finish the branches with a satin stitch to fill the flower buds.
5. Remove any stabilizers, and add soft-touch interfacing to the back of the embroidery (optional).

Summer

1. Transfer the pattern to your collar and stabilize if necessary.
2. Begin this design by embroidering the flowers: Fill both the petals and flower center with a satin stitch. For the petals, it's easiest to start at the outer edges of the petal and bring your stitches in to the center.
3. Next, stitch the bee. Take your yellow floss and place a vertical satin stitch on his body. To create the stripes, use black floss to place a row of stitches directly on top of your previously laid yellow satin stitch, placing each stitch vertically. Don't worry about making your stitches perfectly uniform. Finish the bee's body by embroidering his head with a satin stitch and his legs with a backstitch.

Cont. on page 131

Spring

Backstitch
4 strands,
310

Satin Stitch
4 strands,
3777

Satin Stitch
4 strands,
310

Leaf Satin Stitch
4 strands, 3053

Satin Stitch
4 strands, 3771

Backstitch
4 strands, 3053

Summer

Satin Stitch
4 strands, 21

Satin Stitch
4 strands, 352

Leaf Satin Stitch
4 strands, 890

Satin Stitch
4 strands, 728

Backstitch
4 strands,
890

Satin Stitch
4 strands, 310

Satin Stitch
4 strands, 712

Satin Stitch
4 strands, 3756

Long and Short Stitch
4 strands, 310

Long and Short Stitch
4 strands, 728

Backstitch
4 strands, 310

Fall

Stem Stitch
4 strands,
648

Backstitch
4 strands,
310

Satin Stitch
4 strands,
310

Winter

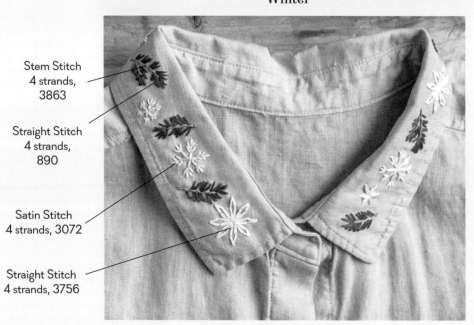

Stem Stitch
4 strands,
3863

Straight Stitch
4 strands,
890

Satin Stitch
4 strands, 3072

Straight Stitch
4 strands, 3756

Cont. from page 128

Winter

4. The bee's wings are two different colors; the top wing uses cream-colored thread, and the lower uses a pale blue. Use each color to place a horizontal satin stitch on the wings, starting your stitches at the outer edges and ending them at the narrowest point (interior) of the wings.

5. Moving on to the leaves, fill them with a leaf satin stitch and backstitch the stems.

6. Finish the summer branches by filling in the flower buds with a satin stitch.

7. Remove any stabilizers, and add soft-touch interfacing to the back of the embroidery (optional).

Fall

1. Transfer the pattern to your collar and stabilize if necessary.

2. Stitch the spider by filling his body with a horizontal satin stitch and his legs with two rows of backstitches. (A row on each leg outline will fill the legs nicely.)

3. Embroider the spider web using a stem stitch, starting with the top of the web and then stitching the three main vertical strands. When the main strands are all embroidered, stitch the remaining sections of the web.

4. Remove any stabilizers, and add soft-touch interfacing to the back of the embroidery (optional).

1. Arrange the motifs in a way that works for your collar, and stabilize if necessary.

2. Stitch the large snowflakes using straight stitches, with one stitch placed between each intersecting line. The smallest snowflake is filled using a satin stitch: In each segment, place a single stitch down the middle and then an additional stitch on each side. The snowflakes are embroidered with two different shades of pale blue—I alternated the placement of each color.

3. Embroider the pine branches by first stem stitching the branches and then adding one or two straight stitches on each line to create the pine needles. I alternated one and two stitches to give the branches a less uniform result.

4. Remove any stabilizers, and add soft-touch interfacing to the back of the embroidery (optional).

romantic rose bralette

Embroidering on a delicate garment like a bralette takes an equally delicate touch, but the results are certainly worth it. With most modern-day bralettes, you will be working with exceptionally stretchy materials, so you'll want to stabilize the inside of the garment. Most importantly, you'll likely have to accept a few wrinkles and creases around your embroidery.

If your bralette will see a lot of wear, I highly recommend you add soft-touch interfacing to the interior when the stitchwork is complete. This will keep the interior embroidery, which is often quite messy, from rubbing against sensitive areas. In my opinion, beauty without comfort simply isn't worth it.

A note on bra sizing: I originally planned on stitching both a rose and fern on each cup, but I ended up using my own bralette for this project and the cup size was too small to fit both. One size certainly does not fit all when it comes to bra-wearing people, so if your bralette is larger than mine (a medium), you'll find the pattern for this project includes an option to stitch both designs on each cup.

Materials

- Bralette
- Transfer tools
- 4-inch (10 cm) embroidery hoop (if garment thickness allows)
- Backing stabilizer (optional)
- DMC embroidery floss
- Embroidery needle
- Embroidery scissors
- Soft-touch interfacing (optional)

Color Guide

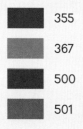

355

367

500

501

Pattern

Page 155

Instructions

1. Transfer the pattern to your bralette and hoop your pattern, or stabilize fabric if necessary.
2. Embroider the fern by filling the leaves with a leaf satin stitch, and then backstitch the stems and branches.
3. Begin the rose by satin stitching the petals on the main flower. It's easiest to fill the inside petals first, then work your way outward. When placing each stitch, begin stitch at the top of the petal and end at the base.
4. When you've stitched the main rose, fill the small bud with a satin stitch.
5. Next, embroider the leaves by filling each leaf with a leaf satin stitch. Make sure to fill the greenery under the small bud as well.
6. When the leaves are filled you can add the veins as an accent. Take your accent color and place a single straight stitch down the center of the leaf, then add some diagonal stitches starting from the outside of the leaf and ending at the center line.
7. Finish the rose by backstitching the stem with the same shade of green you used for the leaves.
8. Remove your hoop and any stabilizers, and add soft-touch interfacing to the back of the embroidery (optional).

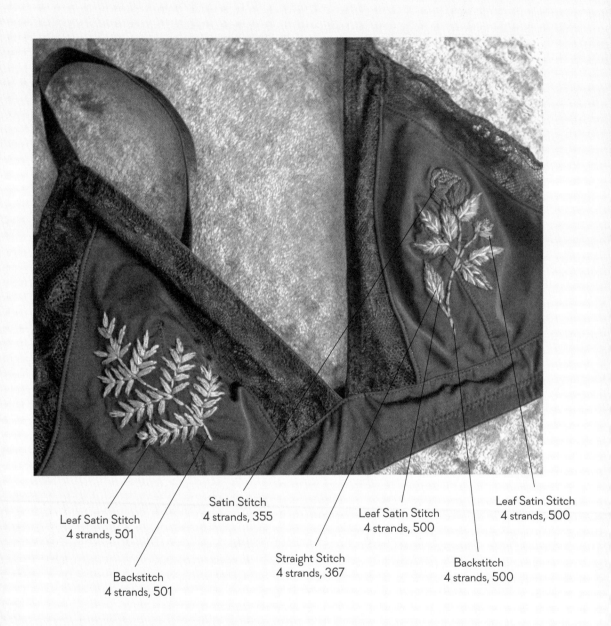

Leaf Satin Stitch
4 strands, 501

Backstitch
4 strands, 501

Satin Stitch
4 strands, 355

Straight Stitch
4 strands, 367

Leaf Satin Stitch
4 strands, 500

Backstitch
4 strands, 500

Leaf Satin Stitch
4 strands, 500

patterns

This section is where you will find the patterns that correspond with the projects in the previous chapter. All you need to do is use your newly acquired pattern-transfer skills, and get started! Patterns are at 100 percent unless marked otherwise.

plain cotton tee, two ways

celestial cardigan

cacti ball cap

floral sweater

wildflower skirt

flourishing jean jacket

witchy dress

witchy dress, continued

woodland sneakers

houseplant jean patch

market bag

market bag, continued

crystal blazer

147

gardener's apron

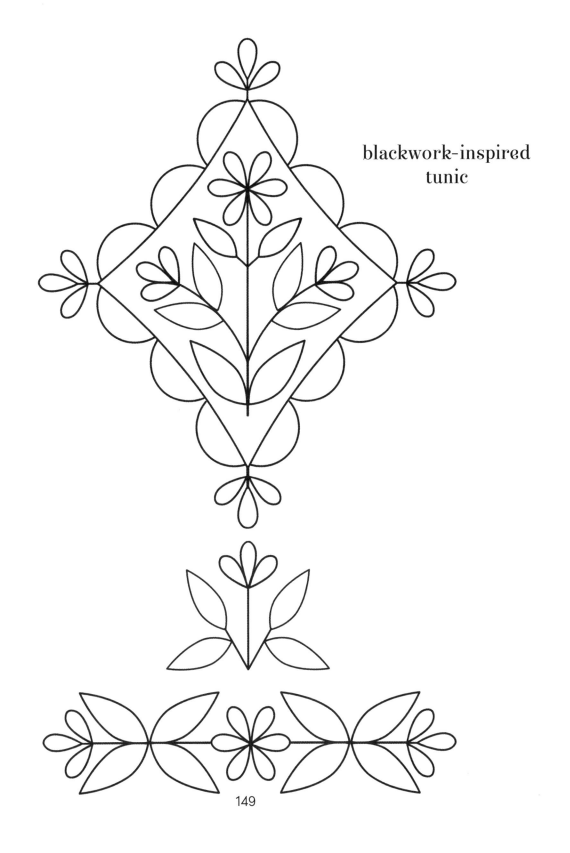

blackwork-inspired
tunic

folky moth camisole

folky moth camisole, continued

greenhouse backpack

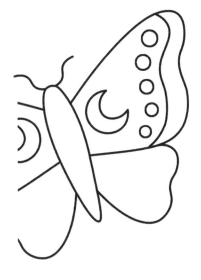

152

harvest bandana,
continued

four collars for
four seasons

spring

four collars for
four seasons, continued

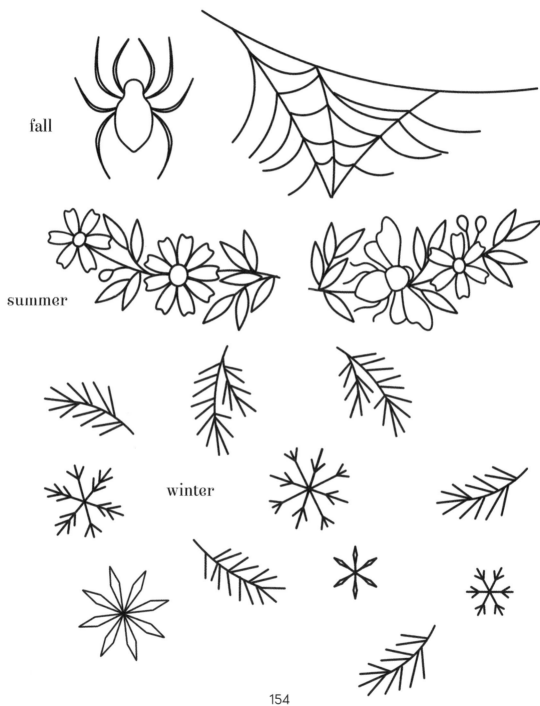

fall

summer

winter

romantic rose
bralette

acknowledgments

riting this book has been one of the greatest privileges of my life. To be able to share my craft with the world in such a way is an honor, one that wouldn't have been possible without the support of many people.

Thank you to Abrams and my wonderful editor, Meredith Clark, for believing in my vision and pushing me beyond my creative comfort zone. I'm unbelievably proud of the projects in this book, and I owe that to you.

To Sean, my best friend and biggest supporter: I've rewritten this paragraph multiple times because I can't quite figure out how to express my gratitude in a way that words can express. Thank you for devoting your time, driving, parenting and housework skills, and emotional support to my book journey. You're the first to remind me I can do hard things, and sometimes I actually believe you. Most importantly, thank you for never once rolling your eyes when I impulsively decide to take on another huge project like starting an embroidery company or writing a book.

To Patricia and Sheena, for pushing me to start this project. If you hadn't answered the phone on the day I called with a wild idea about writing a book, it wouldn't have happened. During the writing process, you have inspired and encouraged me every step of the way. Thank you.

Michelle, my best pal—you have listened to every idea and issue that accompanied the writing of this book, and you did so without judgment or ridicule. Thank you for dropping everything more than once to help me with "book stuff," and for being my biggest cheerleader and my casual therapist.

To my friend Danielle, for your support and excitement about this book. Thank you for encouraging me when I needed it most, and for listening to all my ideas, both good and bad.

To my agent, Stephanie Winter— since day one you've rooted and fought for me. You took a partially formed idea and helped me craft it into a book that surpasses my wildest dreams. Thank you for helping me to find my voice, for believing in me, for all the hand-holding, and for removing all the exclamation marks from my book proposal.

Jenna Hobbs, my wonderful photographer—thank you for loaning me your patience, your skills, your clothes, and your beautiful and creative mind. You are magic, and I'm grateful for this opportunity to get to know you and to call you a friend. And to my models Esmahan and Jessica, thank you for devoting your time and bodies to this book.

To my network of internet friends and supporters across the world: I wouldn't have a business if it weren't for you! Thank you for supporting my craft and keeping the love of fiber art alive.

A special thanks to Pyne and Smith Clothiers and The Skinny for donating garments for me to stitch on, and to DMC embroidery for supplying the tools for this book. Partnerships like this help to keep small businesses like mine alive.

about the author

Alexandra is a self-taught fiber artist living and working in Canada with a passion for sharing her skills and knowledge.

When her son was little, Alexandra found herself longing for an inexpensive creative outlet that could be picked up and put down quickly in the stolen moments of free time that parenthood so rarely affords. She picked up her first needle and fell in love with the textures and colors of embroidery. As she learned technique and developed her style, personal projects turned into gifts, which turned into commission requests, and six months later she started her embroidery business: Florals and Floss.

Fast forward to today: Alexandra now has a thriving business selling embroidery patterns, kits, and her own line of embroidery products, tools, and accessories. A large part of her business is devoted to teaching both beginner embroidery and clothing embroidery workshops at Fern's School of Craft, where some of Alberta's most dedicated textile artists teach modern textile art. FSOC has become a home away from home for Alex, with teaching offering a meaningful way to engage with her community and bring people together over a love of craft and color.

In recent years, Alexandra has taken an interest in the environmental and ethical impact of the garment industry. She loves slow, sustainable, and ethical fashion. However, her budget does not always love the price tag attached. As a way to responsibly source clothes for embroidery, she's taken to thrifting. Buying secondhand can be like going on a treasure hunt, but it's worth the time and energy when you score a cute jean jacket for five dollars!

Alexandra lives in Edmonton, Alberta, with her husband and two young children: a six-year-old budding mycologist who knows everything about everything, and a two-year-old who enjoys climbing on furniture and destroying houseplants. When she isn't embroidering, you'll find her drinking coffee, catching a movie with friends, collecting houseplants, and forcing her family to listen to Broadway soundtracks.

Editor: Meredith A. Clark
Designer: Darilyn Lowe Carnes
Managing Editor: Annalea Manalili
Production Manager: Kathleen Gaffney

Library of Congress Control Number: 2022933504

ISBN: 978-1-4197-5884-3
eISBN: 978-1-64700-540-5

Copyright © 2022 Alexandra Stratkotter
Photography by Jenna Hobbs

Cover © 2022 Abrams

Printed and bound in China
10 9 8 7 6 5 4 3 2 1

Abrams books are available at special discounts when purchased in quantity
for premiums and promotions as well as fundraising or educational use.
Special editions can also be created to specification. For details, contact
specialsales@abramsbooks.com or the address below.

Abrams® is a registered trademark of Harry N. Abrams, Inc.

ABRAMS The Art of Books
195 Broadway, New York, NY 10007
abramsbooks.com